SEP 1 4 2011

MYTHS AND MYSTERIES SERIES

MYTHS AND MYSTERIES

OF

CALIFORNIA

TRUE STORIES
OF THE UNSOLVED AND UNEXPLAINED

RAY JONES WITH JOE LUBOW

Guilford, Connec

Map by Daniel Lloyd © Morris Book Publishing, LLC
Layout: Joanna Beyer
Project editor: Meredith Dias

Library of Congress Cataloging-in-Publication Data is available on file.

ISBN 978-0-7627-6369-6

Printed in the United States of America

10 9 8 7 6 5 4 3 2 1

CONTENTS

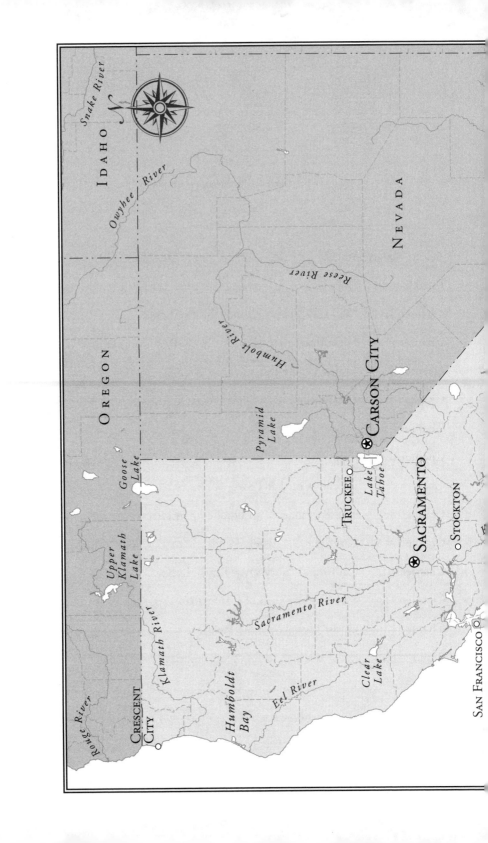

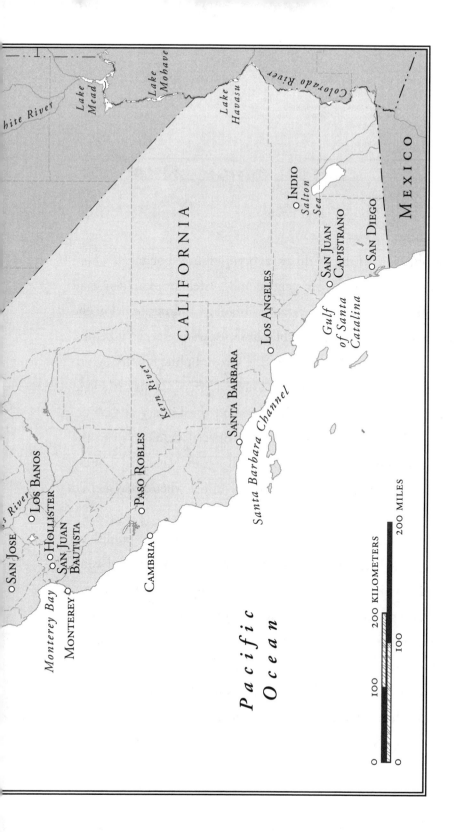

ACKNOWLEDGMENTS

Ray Jones:

The librarians of the world are a forgotten breed of angels whose assistance to humanity in general and writers in particular is all too often ignored. The reference librarians and personnel of the following university and public libraries were especially helpful in the creation of this book: Pacific Grove Public Library, Monterey Public Library, San Jose Public Library, Henry Madden Library at Fresno State University, and the Library at California State University Monterey Bay. Special thanks also to the past and present personnel of Washington Memorial Library in Macon, Georgia, whose generosity to me when I was a child practically forced me to become a writer.

Likewise often ignored are the editors of the publishing houses that package and sell the books that authors feel compelled to write and, if we are lucky, readers purchase and devour. These long-suffering people put up with a lot from writers, many of whom are slow to produce the manuscripts they have promised, not to mention cranky and overly fond of their own words. This particular author hopes that he is not like that, at least not most of the time. And just in case the opposite is true, he would like to express his thanks and sincere appreciation to the entire staff of Globe Pequot Press. Globe Pequot editors Erin Turner and Meredith Rufino deserve special mention for their extraordinary diligence and patience. Thanks.

Joe Lubow:

Like Ray, I am also heavily indebted to the libraries of California, America, and the world. I especially want to thank the staff of the Library at California State University Monterey Bay for its help, since so many of the materials I relied upon came from the collection, databases, and access to the Interlibrary Loan System. I also drew heavily from materials of the Californiana collections of the Monterey Public Library and the Santa Cruz Public Libraries, as well as the Monterey County Free Libraries. Thanks to my old friend Allen Spiegel, who is responsible for bringing Ray and me together, a meeting which has resulted in our collaboration on several writing projects and on the golf course. For their personal support and uplifting spirits, my sister, Marsha Lubow, and my life partner, Tran Ngoc Angie, I also express my everlasting gratitude.

INTRODUCTION

California is a myth and a mystery. People believe things about the Golden State that are not literally true, for instance, that when the next big earthquake hits, the whole place may just drop off into the Pacific. This is a myth, of course, but many think it will happen someday.

Enrico Caruso, the great early twentieth-century opera star, almost certainly believed the state was poised on the brink of oblivion—and for good reason. Fearing that Mt. Vesuvius was about to blow its stack, Caruso canceled a scheduled 1906 performance in Italy and accepted an invitation to sing in California instead. As a result he was thrown out of bed in his San Francisco hotel room when the city was all but destroyed by one of the most powerful earthquakes in history. Sure that the demons beneath Vesuvius had pursued him all the way to California, the tenor leaned out his window to comfort frightened quake victims with a lovely aria and then got out of town as quickly as possible.

Early European explorers apparently believed California had already broken away from the North American continent and drifted out into the Pacific. They thought California was an island, and they had maps to prove it. They also thought it was populated by Amazon women who had so much gold that they used it to make harnesses for the raging wild beasts they employed as mounts.

Sarah Winchester, the extraordinarily wealthy widow of the man who manufactured the "Gun That Won the West," thought California might be a good place to hide from the ghosts of all the thousands of Indians and Confederate soldiers who had been killed by her husband's rifle. The ghosts followed her to San Jose anyway, so she built an enormous mansion to house them. Although Sarah herself has been dead for almost a century, her 160-room "Mystery House" still stands, and visitors often come away convinced that it is still haunted.

Instead of a mystery house, the newspaper tycoon William Randolph Hearst had a mystery yacht. Noted Roaring Twenties producer Thomas Ince is thought by some to have been murdered while attending his own birthday celebration aboard Hearst's palatial party boat, the *Oneida*. Charlie Chaplin and famed silent movie actress Marion Davies were aboard at the time of the incident, which neither they nor Hearst were ever willing to discuss publicly.

The legend of Zorro, the masked and caped hero of Spanish colonial times, is one of California's best-known and best-loved myths, but his story is based in part on that of a real man. During the Gold Rush, Joaquin Murrieta rode the Sierra foothills in the company of four other bandits—all of them named Joaquin—and together they are said to have stolen from the rich and given to the poor in finest Robin Hood style. The California rangers finally put an end to this nonsense, cut off Murrieta's head, and stuffed it into a pickle jar. The mystery of the thing is that the jar eventually disappeared, and no one knows for sure what happened to it.

Another California myth and mystery with links to the era of Spanish rule is the so-called "Lost Ship of the Desert." There are those who say that the shifting sands of the Colorado Desert in southeastern California hide the remains of a Spanish galleon loaded with treasure. Supposedly, the ship was swept far inland and stranded during a flood.

Perhaps the most terrible myth associated with California is the notion that the state was settled in part by cannibals. Some believe that members of the pioneer Donner Party were forced to live off human flesh during the terrible winter of 1846–1847. What these unfortunate people ate or did not eat in no way diminishes the human drama and tragedy of their experiences or the mystery of how and why they became trapped in the Sierras.

California winters are almost never severe except in the mountains, but summers can be extremely dry. In years past long droughts turned crops prematurely brown and caused the water taps of thirsty city dwellers to run dry. People's fondest wish was a means of turning on the rain, and legendary rainmaker Charles Hatfield said he could do just that. The question is, could he really? San Diego officials surely thought so and offered him a fat reward if he would fill municipal reservoirs. According to legend,

Hatfield was so successful that he flooded out the city, and as a result, his employers refused to pay him.

Farmers in the Mussel Slough district of the San Joaquin Valley could have used a little of Hatfield's rain to cool them off way back in 1880 when they were locked in a heated dispute with the railroads over who actually owned their property. The quarrel eventually led to a bloody quick-draw shootout between settlers and representatives of the railroads who were trying to foreclose on their farms. Nobody knows who shot first or why, only that seven men were killed in one of the Old West's legendary gunfights.

In World War II, many years after Mussel Slough, antiaircraft gunners in Los Angeles had a legendary shootout of their own, but to this day no one knows who they were fighting. It wasn't the Japanese because there were no Imperial Navy airplanes over California that night. Some think the intruder that attracted their attention—and as many as 1,400 high-explosive shells—was an alien spacecraft. Others say it was just a weather balloon.

According to popular belief, the gods of old were actually aliens who came to earth in spaceships like the one said by some to have appeared over Los Angeles that night during the 1940s. Others believe that certain gods may have started out as wise and holy men and were later revered and elevated to the status of gods because of their teachings. During the early nineteenth century, Southern California Indians told an old Spanish priest about just such a wise being. Who—or what—was this being, and what became of him?

Guidance of lost souls comes in many forms. The navigational lights established along the California coast beginning in the 1850s have saved countless ships and lives. During the last 150 years, more than a few of these venerable lighthouses have been torn down or bowled over by wind and earthquakes. Even so, some mariners say these lights have not been altogether extinguished and on dark or stormy nights, when their assistance is most needed, they are still tended by ghostly keepers.

All of the stories, myths, and mysteries mentioned above—and more—are detailed in the following chapters. Each of these dramatic tales asks questions that readers must answer for themselves. To seek the solutions, they must enter a realm where reality and truth are not always the same. This place is called the imagination.

CHAPTER 1

Will California Fall into the Pacific?

Perhaps the most widespread and persistent myths associated with California concern the impermanence of the place. Some believe that California is poised on the brink of forever and, when the next mighty earthquake strikes, the entire state, or most of it anyway, will break away from the North American continent and fall off into the vast abyss of the Pacific. It may be that some conservatives, who derisively refer to California as the "left coast," only wish that California would disappear into the Pacific. It is not about to do so any time soon, however, at least not according to the world-renowned seismologists and geologists at the University of Southern California, the California Institute of Technology, and elsewhere, who are paid to know about such things. But are the experts right? Is California's seemingly shaky grip on the West Coast of the United States a permanent state of affairs? There are many who believe it is not.

Phillip McKinnon is a trained engineer, a close acquaintance of the authors, and it is important to add, an inveterate

Easterner. Phillip once said that under no circumstances would he visit California unless it was in a helicopter hovering just above the ground. That way he would be safe and sound when the "big one" hit and the rocks and soil below began to crumble and sink into the Pacific. Since taking this stand more than a decade ago, Phillip has relented and traveled to the West on three separate occasions to enjoy the fun, sun, and golf, and the companionship of friends on California's Monterey Peninsula. On none of these occasions did Phillip engage the services of a helicopter pilot, only those of the pilot supplied at no extra charge by the airline that brought him here. Phillip is very happy indeed that California remained intact during each of his visits and that it didn't fall into the Pacific. However, he is still not sure that it won't.

Many people are convinced that California is an exceptionally dangerous place and that, if you only wait long enough, something terrible is bound to happen here. Actually, they've got that about right. Terrible things do happen in California—forest fires, droughts, floods, mudslides, and tsunamis, to mention a few, and oh yes, earthquakes.

All of these terrible things happen in other places, too. It's just that, in California, the scale is often so much larger. In California mudslides have buried whole neighborhoods, indeed, entire towns. Raging wildfires have consumed not just whole forests, but entire regions of the state. A single California flood in 1905 inundated the better part of the Imperial Valley creating a lake so large that one could not see across it and that for many years was patrolled by the

U.S. Coast Guard. Today, more than a century since the flood, the lake is still there and is referred to as the Salton Sea.

As disasters go, however, there's not much that can compare with a California earthquake. Baseball fans are likely to remember the October 17, 1989, Loma Prieta quake that shook the living daylights out of San Francisco shortly before what was to have been the third game of the World Series between the San Francisco Giants and the Oakland Athletics. Viewers all across the country were watching the pregame telecast as the ball park began to rock and roll, sportscasters began to shout, and the screen went blank. Some may have thought that California had, indeed, at long last plunged into the yawning Pacific. It hadn't, of course, but the damage was severe enough. The 6.9 Richter scale temblor knocked down freeway overpasses, ripped apart a span of the Bay Bridge, and all but destroyed downtown Santa Cruz. It also killed 63 people and injured another 3,737. The Giants and Athletics finally played their third game after a ten-day delay, the longest in series history. The series was ultimately won by Oakland in a four-game sweep, a result that many in San Francisco regarded as a disaster more than equal to the earthquake itself.

Earthquakes like the one in 1989 are said to strike the San Francisco area about once in a lifetime or about every seventy or eighty years. The wait was just a little longer this time. The last time the city was upended by a big temblor was almost exactly eighty-three years and six months earlier, and on that occasion, it was one for the ages. The Italian opera star Enrico Caruso, who some believe was the greatest tenor of all time, could testify to its awful destructiveness.

On the evening of April 17, 1906, Caruso had taken the stage at the ornate San Francisco Opera House to deliver a spellbinding performance as Don José in Bizet's *Carmen*. Caruso's charisma and the extraordinary quality of his voice caused women in his audiences to faint. Doctors were kept on hand with smelling salts to revive them. No doubt many of the ladies present on this particular evening swooned, for by all accounts, Caruso outdid himself, reaching new heights in both volume and tone. It is said that Caruso's voice was so powerful that it could shatter crystal and damage the hearing of anyone who stood too close while he was singing. One might imagine that on this occasion the tenor's high notes not only cracked the goblets of those sipping wine in the wings of the theater but also put asunder the stone deep in the bowels of the earth. Scientists are unlikely to accept the latter theory, but it is a fact that a few hours after Caruso gave his performance, the land to the west of the San Andreas Fault near San Francisco shifted northward in a single mighty lurch. This resulted in a calamity such as few in California or elsewhere have ever witnessed. The earthquake caught Caruso in bed in his luxurious hotel room. He would later describe the event in a magazine article.

On the Wednesday morning early I wake up about 5 o'clock, feeling my bed rocking as though I am in a ship on the ocean, and for a moment I think I am dreaming. Then, as the rocking continues, I get up and go to the window, raise the shade and look out. And what I see makes me tremble with fear. I see the buildings toppling over, big pieces of masonry falling, and from the street below I hear the cries and screams of men and women and children.

I remain speechless, thinking I am in some dreadful nightmare, and for something like 40 seconds I stand there, while the buildings fall and my room still rocks like a boat on the sea. And during that forty seconds I think of 40,000 different things. All that I have ever done in my life passes before me.

Then I gather my faculties together and call for my valet. He comes rushing in quite cool, and, without any tremor in his voice, says: It is nothing. But all the same he advises me to dress quickly and go into the open, lest the hotel fall and crush us to powder. By this time the plaster on the ceiling has fallen in a great shower, covering the bed and the carpet and the furniture, and I, too, begin to think it is time to get busy.

That is precisely what Caruso did. He got very busy indeed searching for a way out of San Francisco. He soon found one, a steamboat that he scurried aboard vowing never to return to this "terrible place."

Interestingly enough, Caruso had come to San Francisco in the first place to avoid a natural disaster. Originally, he had been scheduled to appear that spring in a series of operas in his native

The great San Francisco Earthquake of 1906 may not have dumped California into the Pacific, but it demolished much of the city and killed perhaps as many as three thousand people. Most of the destruction was caused not by the powerful shaking, but by the raging fires that came after the quake. As shown in this photograph, taken a few days after the earthquake, little but charred and broken walls remained of a once-vibrant city..

Italy. The tenor canceled these performances when he heard there had been rumblings beneath Mt. Vesuvius near Naples. The infamous volcano had destroyed Pompeii during Roman times, and apparently the fiery demons within it had reawakened. Caruso therefore prudently accepted an invitation to sing in California instead. In fact, he was in San Francisco when he learned that Vesuvius had indeed erupted. No doubt at the time he congratulated himself on having made a wise decision and remained smug about it right up until 5:13 a.m. on April 18. Afterward, Caruso would bitterly grumble that the subterranean demons of Italy had pursued him across both the Atlantic Ocean and the North American continent. Now he desperately sought to escape them once and for all.

Likely as not, everyone who happened to be in San Francisco on that fateful April morning wished they could do as Caruso did and get out of the city as quickly as possible. The notion that demons resided below the streets of the city may not have seemed at all farfetched to them for they had experienced a terrible shaking. The earthquake was among the most powerful ever felt along the West Coast of the United States. The vibrations are estimated to have reached 7.9 on the open-ended Richter scale. No one knows for sure because the shaking was so violent that it destroyed the instruments scientists had designed and built to measure the strength of earthquakes.

The 1906 San Francisco earthquake is believed to have been at least ten times more powerful than the earthquake that would hit the city eight decades later during the 1989 World Series. It was strong enough to knock down large buildings, rip up city streets, and damage many thousands of structures beyond all hope of repair. By the time the trembling stopped, less than a minute after it had begun, hundreds, if not thousands of San Franciscans lay dead in the rubble. In order to minimize public anxiety, the official death toll was put at 478, a number that most observers at the time recognized as preposterously low.

Among the many myths associated with the earthquake is the belief that most of the damage was caused by the shaking. Actually, far greater destruction was caused by the fire that came after the earthquake. You see, the city that had stood on the San Francisco Peninsula in the middle of April 1906 was made of wood—redwood to be exact. Old San Francisco had been built with countless millions of board-feet of lumber drawn from the mighty sequoia forests to the north. Redwood is strong, resistant to decay, handsome, and aromatic and, during the late nineteenth century, it was also very plentiful and cheap. Despite its advantages, however, redwood is profoundly vulnerable to fire. In the wild, sequoia trees are protected by a fire-retardant cloak of shaggy bark. That, in part, is why these giant trees sometimes live for thousands of years. But once stripped of its bark and cut into planks, the fragrant reddish wood of the coastal sequoia burns like kindling. In effect, early twentieth-century San Francisco was a mighty bonfire waiting to be set aflame, and the earthquake struck the match. Almost before the shaking had stopped, hundreds of small fires were touched off by ruptured gas mains, overturned oil lamps, collapsed chimneys, and red hot coals spilled out onto tinder-dry wooden floors. Soon these individual fires began to join forces, and eventually they merged into a single mighty conflagration that began to consume the city block by flaming block.

San Francisco's fire-fighting forces had been decapitated at the outset when Fire Chief Dennis Sullivan was struck down by falling masonry during the earthquake. Efforts to combat the blaze were further hampered as broken water mains rendered fire hoses useless in many parts of the city. Having turned the commercial buildings, hotels, and warehouses in the business district into giant torches, the fire then marched westward into the sprawling San Francisco residential neighborhoods. Hot easterly winds, some of them whipped up by the flames themselves, created a firestorm that incinerated as many as a thousand structures every hour.

For three days, frantic firefighters, their ranks increased by soldiers from the San Francisco Presidio and desperate citizens struggling to save their neighborhoods, fell back before the advancing inferno. Then, at the broad north-south thoroughfare of Van Ness Avenue, they decided to make their last stand. If the fire could not be stopped here, then nothing of the city could be saved. In hopes of creating a fire break, Army Corps of Engineers demolition experts, who had been pressed into service as firemen, began to dynamite houses on the east side of Van Ness. In some cases, the owners were given less than ten minutes to pack their belongings and get out. Meanwhile fire crews pumped frantically to hose down the roofs of houses just west of the avenue. Not long afterward the bright red wall of fire swept down the hill toward Van Ness. People cried out and prayed as it closed in on them. The flames sputtered. Then it began to rain.

Of course San Francisco is not the only place in California that is prone to big earthquakes. Most of the state is highly susceptible to temblors, and many California towns and cities get a severe shaking every few decades. Particularly vulnerable is San Juan Bautista, a historic community about 80 miles south of San Francisco.

The Mission San Juan Bautista was established near the end of the eighteenth century to provide a convenient resting place along the Camino Real, a rough dirt track—little more than a footpath really—that linked the missions in San Diego, Santa Barbara, Carmel, and San Francisco. The stopover was not just used by monks, though. It became popular with prospectors, miners, cowboys, merchants, and travelers of every sort, and in time, a little town grew up beside the mission.

Driving into town, one gets the impression that not very much has changed here. San Juan Bautista's one commercial street is chockablock with rustic bars, restaurants, and wood or adobe buildings of just the sort one associates with nineteenth-century California prospectors, cowboys, and miners. It gives visitors the feeling that had they arrived here, say, 150 years ago on a horse, the place would have looked exactly the same. As attractive as that notion may be, it is, alas, a mistaken one. San Juan Bautista's very old-looking buildings have been built, rebuilt, and repaired repeatedly. At the mission it is easy to see why this is the case.

The Mission San Juan Bautista with its 230-foot-long brick colonnade dominates the entire north side of California's last surviving Spanish plaza. The west and south sides of the plaza are occupied by old wooden government buildings, hotels, and livery stables, all of which have been restored and opened to the public as museums. On the fourth side there are no buildings at all for here the ground drops down into a tree-lined gully, and running through it is that wayfarers' wonder, the Camino Real. Something else runs through the gully as well, for between the Camino and the plaza with its stone and adobe church is that notorious crack in the earth called the San Andreas Fault.

Stretching out beyond the fault, the Camino, and the mission is a breathtaking expanse of flat fields planted as far as the horizon with artichokes, tomatoes, lettuce, and it would seem, every conceivable variety of garden vegetable. The prodigious fertility of these lands likely accounts for the selection of San Juan Bautista as the site for the mission. It was the fifteenth of those established by Franciscan padres when Spain ruled California.

When the mission was founded in 1797, the Franciscans sent a pair of priests here to build a church and Christianize the local Indians. Obediently, Fathers Jose Manuel Martiarena and Pedro Adriano Martínez hiked here along the rugged Camino and founded a mission. Looking down at the Camino today, it is awe-inspiring to think that for early mission monks like Martínez and Martiarena this dusty lane served as their one and only link to the outside world. Every scrap of news they received from Monterey, about a week's walk to the south, or from the far more distant San Diego, Mexico, or Spain, came by way of the Camino. But however little they may have known of the world, they knew even less about the earth itself. Otherwise, they would never have put a mission in a place like San Juan Bautista. What they didn't know and, of course, couldn't have known, was that the ground beneath their feet was on the move. The salad fields seen nowadays to the east of the mission are moving south along with the rest of North America. The mission and the town, not to mention Monterey, Los Angeles, and a sizable chunk of the continent-sized Pacific Plate, are moving north. All this shifting about stretches the rocks, and inevitably something gives. Then the earth begins to rock and roll.

The mission received its first severe shaking just one year after it was established. The priests shrugged off this setback, repairing damaged structures and continuing with their work of converting the Indians to Christianity and the local fields to farmland. But there was more to come—much more. In October 1800 the ground under the mission once more started to tremble, and this time the shaking seemed as if it would never stop. Several severe earthquakes rumbled through the area, each of them followed by as many as six sharp aftershocks. Roofs fell, adobe walls crumbled to dust, and the earth itself split open.

The quakes not only shattered mission buildings but also the seemingly indomitable spirit of Father Martínez, who moved his cot out into the open under the stars. No amount of reassurance or persuasion could convince the good priest to reenter any of the mission buildings even after they had been repaired. Eventually, he was reassigned to another mission. Likely Martínez considered himself fortunate to have escaped San Juan Bautista with his life, but had he understood the true nature of California's fractured geology, he might have done as Caruso would later do: board a ship and leave the region all together.

No place in California is safe from earthquakes, but San Juan Bautista may be among the *least* safe. Major quakes or groups of quakes have struck the mission and the town no fewer than six times over the last two centuries. Of course, there have always been other threats. Indians sometimes attacked the mission. On one such occasion, the mission priests drove off a sizable war party by dragging the church organ out into the plaza and playing it at full blast.

Unfortunately, the same technique could not be used to restrain the warriors—some might call them demons—below the earth. Repeatedly damaged by temblors large and small, the mission was all but destroyed during the San Francisco Earthquake of 1906. Even though the epicenter of the quake was more than 80 miles to the north, damage to the mission was so severe that it did not fully recover until the 1950s.

California missions and other historic structures are as vulnerable today as they were centuries ago. The damage caused by twenty-first-century earthquakes is not limited to freeways and sports stadiums. Late in 2003, nearly a century after Caruso made his escape from San Francisco and two centuries after Father Martínez fled San Juan Bautista in terror, the earth unleashed its violence on yet another part of the state. At precisely 56 seconds after 11:15 in the morning on December 22, the first day of winter, two massive rock formations below the mountains east of San Simeon lurched past one another releasing energy equal to several nuclear detonations. In Paso Robles, about 25 miles west of the epicenter, the vibrations were so intense they lique-fied the mortar between bricks causing an entire block of early twentieth-century buildings to collapse. Among them was an old bank with a brick clock tower rising above its entrance. The heavy clock fell into the street crushing a car along with its driver and a passenger.

At the two-hundred-year-old Mission San Miguel just north of Paso Robles, the ferocious shaking caught a lone parishioner inside the lovely old adobe, stone, and timber church. It was three days before Christmas, and Remi Campomensi had volunteered to help prepare for the special holiday services to be held in the mission's ornate sanctuary. She had just started placing wreaths at the foot of sacred statues and stringing greenery along the walls and banisters, when the floor began to move.

At first Remi thought the deafening roar she heard was coming from a train rushing along the tracks across the street from the mission, but quickly realized that something far worse was happening. Candlesticks were toppling over and chunks of decorative plaster were falling from the walls. In terror she stood before a painted statue of the Virgin Mary and started to pray. The statue fell over and its head broke off and rolled across the floor. Even more terrified, she now directed her prayers to a nearby statue of Saint Joseph, but he too fell and was decapitated when he hit the floor. Only one large statue was left, that of the mission's patron, the Archangel Michael, who stood guard over the nave with sword in hand. Remi dared not address the golden archangel for fear that her prayers might bring him down as well. Even though she had stopped praying, the archangel may have granted her wishes anyway, for the shaking soon ceased, and though bits of adobe, plaster, and paint rained from the upper walls and ceiling, the archangel, the church, and Remi remained upright.

For several years following the earthquake, the Christmas decorations and the headless statues of Mary and Joseph remained on the floor of the San Miguel Mission sanctuary exactly where they had fallen. No one was allowed back inside for fear that the earth would begin to tremble once again and complete the destruction of the church, this time with fatal results. Or maybe they were afraid that the earth might split open and the mission along with the entire state of California might slide off into the Pacific. It hasn't happened yet for the mission and the state are still here—at least for the time being.

CHAPTER 2

Is California an Island?

People who don't live in California and many of those who do tend to think of it as a place apart, wholly unlike any other region of North America, or for that matter, the world. They're convinced that the streets are cleaner in California, the lawns neater, and the flowers more colorful. They're sure that California men—and women in particular—are more attractive, their houses more beautiful and spacious, and their parties more lively. In this vision, California is one big Beverly Hills, complete with starlets and expensive shops like the ones on Rodeo Drive, and not far away are mountains sparkling with gold that can be used to pay for everything. And if gold, for some reason, is not available, then there are great jobs in the entertainment and technology industries of Los Angeles or the Silicon Valley that offer enormous salaries and don't require a lot of work. To people who think like this, California is, for all intents and purposes, an island separated from the rest of the planet by oceans of the imagination.

Early Spanish explorers believed California was an island, and European cartographers often depicted it that way on maps and charts like this one drawn in 1650.

California has often been portrayed this way in films that paint an overly sunny picture of the state and of the life people live here. During the Gold Rush, somewhat similar ideas were advertised by unscrupulous steamship lines to sell tickets to San Francisco. However, it was not the movie industry that gave birth to such notions. Nor was it the Gold Rush. People have been thinking this way about California for hundreds of years.

The first explorers who set out in search of California were not afraid that it might drop off the edge of the North American continent and float away into the Pacific. They were sure that it had already done so. They were certain that California was an island, and they had maps to show that this was so.

Many early maps depicted California as detached from the continent with a substantial stretch of ocean separating it from the West Coast of North America. Prepared by some of the finest cartographers of the fifteenth, sixteenth, and seventeenth centuries, these maps were often meticulously drawn and quite handsome. It is hard to say how capable mapmakers got the idea that California was surrounded by water, especially since very few Europeans had ever seen it, but the explanation may lie in a work of fiction.

In 1510, a novelist by the name of Garci Rodriguez de Montalvo published a romance entitled *Las Sergas de Esplandián* or *The Adventures of Esplandián.* In this book, Rodriguez describes the wanderings of a chivalrous hero whose travels take him to a fabulous island called California. Here is what Rodriguez says of this place:

> On the right hand of the Indies is an island called California, very near to the Terrestrial Paradise and inhabited by black women without a single man among them and living in the manner of the Amazons. They are robust of body, strong and passionate of heart, and of great valor. Their island is one of the most rugged in the world with bold rocks and crags. Their arms are all of gold as are the harnesses of the wild beasts, which after taming, they ride. In all the island there is no other metal.

It may be that many of Rodriguez's readers wished his story to be true even if they did not altogether believe it, and in time, their longing turned to conviction. Renaissance-era Europeans became convinced that the island of California definitely did exist. They could envision its mountains rising out of the coastal mists and could see themselves stepping out of a boat onto its golden beaches and reaching down to lift precious jewels out of the surf.

Dreams of this sort drove countless young adventurers to board crowded and, all too often, leaky ships and set sail for America. They knew that Columbus had discovered a large island called Cuba, but there was no gold there, no jewels, and no attractive Amazons. They figured that California with all its wonders must lie elsewhere.

Among the youthful fortune seekers who set sail for the Americas during the early sixteenth century, few were more determined or hungrier for gold and riches than Hernando Cortes. He had read Montalvo's book and may very well have fancied himself a real-life embodiment of the fictional Esplandián. After a brief stopover in Cuba, which he found depressingly poor and totally lacking in the reach-out-and-grab-it sort of riches he sought, Cortes pushed on in search of California.

Accompanied by several hundred like-minded Spanish soldiers of fortune, Cortes landed on the shores of Mexico in February of 1519. Within little more than three years, Cortes' little Spanish army with its cannon and horses had conquered the once mighty Aztec Empire. Although there was no shortage of gold and other sources of wealth in Mexico, it soon became obvious that this was not the place described by Montalvo. Mexico was, after all, not surrounded by water and, like Cuba, it had no warrior women.

Cortes might have begun to wonder if Montalvo had ever seen California or had ever spoken to anyone who had seen it. Nonetheless, Cortes mounted further expeditions to search for the novelist's mythic island. One of these set sail from the west coast of Mexico in about 1536 and soon discovered the thousand-mile-long peninsula known today as Baja California. Although the Spanish did not manage to sail all the way around the peninsula—for the obvious reason that it was not really an island—Cortes believed that here at last he had found California. Surely, somewhere beyond the rocky shores of this rugged place were the strange beasts, muscular black Amazons, and unfathomable riches of which he had dreamed. None of these wonders were ever discovered. Even so, Cortes continued to believe in the fable of California until the day he died near the end of 1547. Others shared his belief, even some prominent European mapmakers.

In 1602, Sebastian Vizcaino sailed up the California coast, and Father Antonio de la Ascension kept a journal of the voyage. Ascension claimed that California was separated from the American continent by the "Mediterranean Sea of California." It is not clear where Ascension got this notion, but in the minds of romantic Europeans, his claim confirmed that California was, in fact, an island. Indeed, maps began to show it that way. Some depicted a coastline bearing a close resemblance to the actual coastal topography of the Baja Peninsula. In the north, however, where the peninsula attaches to the North American continent, these maps showed a broad expanse of ocean. There it was then, in all its glory, the Island of California. But where were the gold beaches and Amazons? Nobody could find them.

As early as 1542, Juan Rodriguez Cabrillo had sailed up the West Coast of North America searching for the Strait of Anian, a mythical passage said to link the Atlantic and Pacific Oceans. Perhaps he also thought he might find Montalvo's island paradise, but if so, he was bitterly disappointed. Cabrillo took his three ships as far north as modern-day Oregon, exploring dozens of inlets and bays along the way. However, not one of them promised to carry him as far eastward as the Atlantic or as far southward as the Gulf of California, known in those days as the Sea of Cortes. If there was no such passage, then California could not possibly be an island, but Cabrillo would not live to conclusively prove the point. He died from wounds he had received in a skirmish with a war party of California Indians—all of them apparently men.

Toward the end of the seventeenth century, a Jesuit missionary known as Father Eusebius Francis Kino set off into the wild desert lands of northwestern Mexico in search of Indian souls to save. Father Kino found only a few Indians in this barren country, but he did make a very significant discovery. Not far from what is today the city of Yuma, Arizona, his trek was halted by a very wide and very muddy river. It was the Colorado, and it flowed into the Gulf of California. There was no channel here breaking through to the Pacific from the north end of the gulf, only the great Colorado pouring down from the mountains and deserts to the north.

It is said that Father Kino rafted across the Colorado on more than one occasion, but the western shore of the river was about as far as he ever got into what is now the state of California. Even so, he had proven rather conclusively that California was not an island. Obviously, it was quite firmly attached to North America. Eventually, frustrated European fortune hunters and misguided mapmakers would reach the same conclusion.

The irony of all this is that California has always lived up to its insular reputation. Although not surrounded by water, California has been and remains to this day encircled by a wreath of mystery. A vast expanse of nearly impassable deserts and a wall of towering, snowy mountains cut California off from the rest of the continent. These barriers have not only made it extremely difficult for people to get into and out of the place, they have given California a unique flora and fauna. For instance, except for a single, small grove of coastal redwoods in southern Oregon, sequoia trees grow nowhere else on the planet. The California condor, California cougar, and countless other animals and plants are unique to the state. And as everyone knows, California produces some fairly unusual people. Stand on a street corner in San Francisco's Mission District or take a walk along Rodeo Drive in Beverly Hills and you are bound to encounter a few of them.

CHAPTER 3

House of Mystery

People taking a tour of the Winchester Mystery House in San Jose would do well to keep a careful count of their companions. Group tours of this gargantuan Victorian mansion may start out with twelve guests and end up with ten, eleven, or even thirteen. The winding, twisting, hour-long tours of the Winchester's maze of hallways, bedrooms, dressing rooms, kitchens, pantries, dining rooms, sitting rooms, conservatories, reception halls, ballrooms, porches, and storage rooms offer ample opportunities to lose someone or to pick up an extra person. It is quite common and understandable for visitors to get lost at the Winchester, and usually they wander around until they bump into—often quite unexpectedly—their own group, the one behind, or the one up ahead. In this way, a group may grow or shrink according to how closely its members trail behind their official guide.

However, there are some who believe that not everyone they've seen at the Winchester is either a paying guest or a

Mystery House employee. Sometimes a workman is sighted dressed in overalls and lugging around an old-fashioned tool box. At other times an old woman wearing a black shawl is seen in one or another of the bedrooms or sitting at a table in the famous Séance Room. Other figures are noticed as well, outfitted in a manner that in no way resembles twenty-first-century dress—or, in some cases, twentieth-century either.

One might get the impression that the Winchester House is one of those so-called living history museums filled with re-enactors dressed in period costume, but it very definitely is not. The Winchester is a museum all right, but one rather more dedicated to the history of the dead.

It should come as no surprise at all that people occasionally get lost at the Winchester—actually, it happens just about everyday—or that they are uncertain as to what they've seen or not seen here. The house is a jumble of 160 rooms stacked several stories high and spread out across more than four acres. It has at least forty bedrooms, thirteen bathrooms, and six separate kitchens all connected by serpentine hallways that sometimes double back upon themselves. It has seventeen chimneys and forty-seven fireplaces, four of them in just one room. Several of the chimneys are not linked to fireplaces or to anything at all. There are ten thousand windows, many of them framing leaded glass or expensive Tiffany art glass. There are fifty-two skylights, some of them installed one atop the other. There are nearly two thousand doors, some of which open onto blank walls or

Built one room at a time over a period of nearly forty years, the Winchester House evolved into an extraordinary labyrinth of hallways and staircases. Some think—and with no shortage of good reason—that this old Victorian mansion is haunted.

dead-end passageways. A few of the doors swing out onto thin air meaning that, if you opened them and stepped over the doorsill, you would fall straight down two stories or more to the ground.

The Winchester's staircases are a marvel unto themselves. Depending on how you count them, there are at least forty staircases, some of them winding round and round and ending up nowhere. The top step may end at a wall or ceiling. Some staircases skip entire floors or provide access to only a single room. One staircase leads up, down, and then back up again. Another consists of forty-four steps, each of them only two inches high. The latter is known today as the Switchback Staircase as it makes seven complete turns. Anyone climbing this staircase travels more than one hundred feet with an overall gain in elevation of only nine feet. The Switchback Staircase is unusual in that nearly all of the other staircases have exactly thirteen steps.

Everywhere one goes in the Winchester House one encounters the number thirteen. For instance, most of the windows have thirteen panes of glass, and the greenhouse features thirteen cupolas. There is a sink with thirteen drains and a chandelier with thirteen lights. Thirteen palm trees line the driveway, and as mentioned earlier, there are thirteen bathrooms. Incidentally, several of the bathrooms are fitted with glass doors!

So what's it all about? There seems to be no rhyme or reason about the place. What was the purpose of such a large house with so many bedrooms, kitchens, and fireplaces? Why the maze of hallways? The bizarre staircases? The doors that open onto nothing? What is the significance of all those repetitions of the number thirteen? One might imagine the house was intended as some sort of asylum. Well it was, in a sense, the asylum and obsession of one very lonely and very rich old woman.

It has been said that within every book resides the spirit of the person who wrote it. Built over a period of nearly four decades during which construction continued around the clock, 365 days a year, the Winchester Mystery House is something like a book with many hundreds, if not thousands of pages. Each chapter and verse testifies to the indomitable and extraordinarily eccentric spirit of a single person. Her name was Sarah L. Winchester.

She was born Sarah Lockwood Pardee in 1840, more than two decades before the beginning of the Civil War. The daughter of New England aristocrats, she had, by most accounts, a happy childhood. Blossoming into a lovely, round-faced girl with cherub cheeks who could play the piano and speak several languages, she no doubt attracted many suitors. The one whose attentions she encouraged was young William Wirt Winchester, the son of Oliver Winchester, a wealthy shirt manufacturer. In 1862 they were married.

During the late 1850s, Oliver Winchester had bought a controlling interest in a New Haven, Connecticut, arms company. Under his guidance it would grow into the Winchester Repeating Arms Company, manufacturer of the famed Winchester rifle, the "Gun That Won the West." Known for its reliability and its ability to kill a buffalo, a bear, or an enemy at considerable range, the sturdy rifle earned the Winchesters an enormous fortune.

When Oliver Winchester died in 1880, William Winchester inherited a sizable portion of his fortune and took over as president of the Winchester Company. He would not hold the position long, however, for the following year he died of consumption, the lung disease known today as tuberculosis. His passing at the early age of forty-three proved a crushing blow to his wife, the former Sarah Pardee. Some years earlier, Sarah had lost an infant daughter to marasmus, a childhood disease that wastes the body until nothing is left but skin and bones and finally the heart stops. Having sunk into a depression from which she would never fully recover, Sarah would have no more children. The loss of her husband in 1881 proved more than she could bear, and it seemed for a while that she might go mad.

At this point the life story of Sarah Winchester becomes shrouded in mystery. We know, of course, where she went and what she did. She moved to California and started work on what was to become one of the world's most extraordinary—and bizarre—structures. For the remaining decades of her life the construction of her home in San Jose would be her obsession. What no one will ever be able to say for sure, however, is why.

Much of what we know about Sarah Winchester from the 1880s onward must be drawn from legend or intuited from the weird and yet strangely beautiful building she left behind when she finally died in 1922. It is said that, desperate to break through the veil of sadness that had fallen over her following the death of her husband, she sought the help of a spiritualist, a medium who claimed to be able to communicate with the dead. According to legend, the medium told her the Winchester family was cursed by the spirits of all the many thousands of people who had been shot and killed by Winchester rifles. These angry ghosts had carried off her husband and would take her as well unless she very carefully followed their instructions. She was told to move to California and start work on a home for the dead. If construction ever ceased, she, too, would die.

In 1884 Sarah appeared in Menlo and within a few months had purchased a stretch of lush farmland in the Santa Clara Valley. The farm had an eight-room house on it, and this was the seed from which her fantastic mansion was to grow, one room at a time, over the next thirty-eight years. Offering $3 a day, double the usual local rate, she hired carpenters and set them to work. Once construction began later that same year, it would continue ceaselessly, twenty-four hours a day, 365 days a year including holidays, through heat, cold, wind, and rain.

She had plenty of money to keep the project going. She had inherited millions from her husband and a 49 percent interest in the Winchester Company. The return on her shares alone amounted to about $1,000 a day or one-third of a million dollars a year in nineteenth-century money—there were practically no taxes back then. Her dividends for just one day would pay one of her workers for a year.

With resources like those, she could afford the best materials and she bought them. The frame and siding of her steadily growing mansion were built with redwood. The parquet floors found in many of the rooms were made of mahogany, teak, maple, oak, and rosewood. Tiffany windows, some of them valued at more than $1,000 each, were brought in and stored until they could be installed in a suitable room. Many were never used at all, but merely sat gathering dust in Sarah's storeroom. The materials and fineries there were valued at $25,000 in 1922, at which time such a sum was considered by most to be a small fortune and was more than sufficient to purchase and furnish a very handsome estate.

Sarah's own mansion was handsome in its trappings, but perhaps not otherwise. It suffered greatly from a lack of any general plan. Over the years it grew amoeba-like, first in one direction then in another, upwards and sideways, in straight lines, squares, rectangles, and ellipses. The Winchester heiress served as her own general contractor, and it seems obvious that she was not guided by any overall architectural vision. How was the house supposed to look when the last nail had been driven and the walls had received their final coat of paint? Apparently, she had no idea. Likely this was so because the legends associated with her are accurate in at least one important respect: Sarah Winchester never intended to complete the project. So, on it went for thirty-eight long years.

Meanwhile, Sarah buried herself in her obsession, constantly ordering new and often very expensive materials and furnishings and giving orders to carpenters, plumbers, floor layers, roofers, painters, and gardeners. (The property had extensive, well-manicured grounds.) She also hid herself within the steadily growing labyrinth of her home. It is said that she rarely slept two consecutive nights in the same bedroom and that she moved about from place to place through secret passageways that had been created, intentionally or otherwise, by the workmen who followed her often haphazard instructions. Some believe that she behaved this way in order to keep one step ahead of the ghosts that haunted the Winchester family and her San Jose estate.

Did Mrs. Winchester really believe her footsteps were dogged by ghosts? Did she believe she was haunted by the spirits of people who had been killed by Winchester rifles and that they would take revenge on her the moment she quit building her house in California? Maybe building the house was merely the strange and very costly hobby of an eccentric old woman. No one will ever know for certain.

What is known for sure is that Sarah was a very private person who never discussed her motives with anyone. In fact, she rarely if ever received visitors. Except for Sarah herself and the small army of phantoms who might or might not have made a home there, the huge house stood empty almost 100 percent of the time. Curious passersby who might have liked a closer look at the mansion, which grew more famous as it grew ever larger year after year, were invariably turned away. No matter how rich, powerful, or well known the people, the door of the Winchester House would not open for them.

According to legend, Sarah's penchant for privacy and her closed-door policy extended even to the president of the United States. During his cowboy days in the Dakotas, Theodore Roosevelt acquired a great affection for the Winchester rifle, so during a presidential visit to California in 1903, he decided to stop off in San Jose and pay his respects to the Winchester widow. He never got past the front door. A workman, who did not know and, perhaps, did not care who he was, supposedly told the president to go around back. Roosevelt then left in a huff.

While Sarah could keep away unwanted visitors—even the likes of a president—her great wealth and determination were not enough to hold at bay the forces of nature. Shortly after five o'clock in the morning on April 18, 1906, the ground beneath nearly the entire state of California began to move backward and forward. In San Francisco the shaking threw opera star Enrico Caruso out of bed while in the process of destroying much of the city. In San Jose, the mighty earthquake also rudely awakened the mistress of the Winchester House, which seemed likely to fall down around her ears. The vibration toppled the mansion's seven-story observation tower and several of its ornate cupolas. Falling timbers and masonry trapped Sarah in the Daisy Bedroom, which she had come to favor over other sleeping quarters in her huge home. After the shaking subsided, her frantic servants and workmen began a thorough search of the property. They did not know where she was, and it would take them several hours to find her and pull her from the debris.

Despite the severe beating it had taken from the earthquake, the house remained structurally sound, and Sarah soon set her builders to work repairing the damage. Interestingly, she also had them wall off the entire front end of the house, including the Daisy Bedroom, so-called because of the bright yellow daisies on its art glass windows. Afterward, she kept this bedroom, the grand ballroom, and approximately thirty other rooms sealed for the remainder of her life.

Sarah Winchester would live and keep workers busy adding new rooms to her house for another sixteen years. Then, on September 5, 1922, Sarah Winchester died of heart failure at the age of eighty-two. The angry ghosts may finally have taken their vengeance on her, but if so, she had held them off for a very long time. According to legend, construction work on the Winchester House ceased immediately upon her death. Some say the work stopped so abruptly that nails were left half-driven and boards left half-sawn.

After she died, Mrs. Winchester's relatives swarmed like locusts over her property in San Jose. Some were said to have been disappointed by the size of her financial holdings, which perhaps not surprisingly, had shrunk over the years. It may be that they hoped to find hidden within the colossal home or buried somewhere on its sprawling grounds riches in gold and silver plate, jewels, bonds, or currency. Apparently, they found very little in the way of bankable wealth. Mrs. Winchester's will, which was written in thirteen sections and signed thirteen times, left the furnishings and other household goods to a niece who had them trucked away to an auction house. It took a large crew of movers six weeks to remove the furniture.

Mrs. Winchester's body was taken back to Connecticut, where she was buried beside her husband and the little girl she had lost so many years before. Once she and her furnishings were gone, legend and rumor moved in behind them. There were those who said she had been a spy and those who said she was stark raving mad. There were stories about the séances she was said to hold nearly every evening. One such story appeared some years after her death in the *American Weekly,* a magazine published by California news tycoon William Randolph Hearst. Here is an excerpt:

> When Mrs. Winchester set out for her séance room, it might well have discouraged the ghost of the Indian or even of the bloodhound to follow her. After traversing an interminable labyrinth of rooms and hallways, suddenly she would push a button, a panel would fly back, and she would step quickly from one apartment into another, and unless the pursuing ghost was watchful and quick, he would lose her. Then she opened a window in that apartment and climbed out, not into the open air, but onto the

top of a flight of steps that took her down one story only to meet another flight that brought her right back up to the same level again, all inside the same house. This was supposed to be very discomforting to evil spirits who are said to be naturally suspicious of traps.

Perhaps the evil spirits eventually left for want of company, but who knows? In time, the Winchester estate became a museum, and it continues to serve that function today. Having been placed on the National Register of Historic Places and declared a California Historical Landmark, the Winchester House has been restored and is very well preserved. More than a few of the rooms have been refurnished with antiques from the Victorian period. The museum receives no public funds, but rather is supported by revenues from the cafe and gift shop on the estate and from ticket sales for tours.

Open to the public every day of the year except Christmas, the Winchester Mystery House offers guided mansion tours that depart every few minutes from the vicinity of the gift shop. The guides point out the endless oddities of the place—the useless doors and chimneys and stairs that lead to nothing in particular—as well as the beautiful woodwork and colorful glass windows and elegant parquet floors. In most cases, however, they leave the spiritual side of things to the varied imaginations of their guests. Even so, visitors can be forgiven if they glance into a room just off one of the long dark hallways and see the indistinct figure of someone who is not necessarily a member of their particular tour group.

The old mansion is, after all, a very eerie place. In fact, it may be one of the spookiest places on the planet. Visitors often report feeling a chill come over them and a tingling sensation in their toes and fingers. They hear voices emanating from the walls and ceilings and crackling sounds arising from stone cold fireplaces. And they are struck by the inescapable sense of not being alone, even when they are, in fact, alone. That is why, at the Winchester, it is always a good idea to keep up with one's group—that and the likelihood of becoming hopelessly, impossibly, and infinitely lost.

So is the Winchester House haunted? Depending on how superstitious you may be, you can answer that question for yourself, but consider this: Even if there are no hobgoblins at the Winchester, no ghosts of Indians and Confederate soldiers who were slaughtered by Winchester rifles, there is still one spirit that hangs about the place and can never be removed from it. That is the spirit of Sarah Winchester. She is a part of every nail and redwood timber, every strip of mahogany, every pane of glass, every stone, and every scrap of tile. She is the soul of the Winchester Mystery House.

CHAPTER 4

Did William Randolph Hearst
Get Away with Murder?

On Saturday, November 15, 1924, a lavish luxury yacht known as the *Oneida* slipped out of San Pedro Harbor in Los Angeles and set sail for San Diego. The 230-foot *Oneida* was a glistening vessel appointed with the finest rare woods and polished fittings, and everything aboard her—from the gold plate and silver in the galley to the nearly priceless carpets in the lounge—was the best that money could buy. In fact, the yacht fairly reeked of money, as one might have expected, since it was owned by newspaper mogul William Randolph Hearst. Money was never much of a problem for Hearst because he could more or less print whatever he needed.

The *Oneida* was especially shipshape as she cruised out into the Pacific that Saturday, for onboard was a who's who of Southern California royalty. Hearst had invited actress Marion Davies, widely known to be his mistress, silent film star Charlie Chaplin, gossip columnist Louella Parsons, author Elinor Glyn,

COURTESY OF THE LIBRARY OF CONGRESS

When this picture was taken shortly before World War I, newspaper tycoon William Randolph Hearst was one of the richest and most powerful men in the world. Some believe that a decade later his love for actress Marion Davies would drive him to kill.

and a bevy of lesser but nonetheless well-known personages. The occasion was a belated birthday celebration for movie producer Thomas Ince who had turned forty-two a few days earlier. Ironically, Ince was not aboard the *Oneida* when she sailed.

Like most successful Hollywood producers, Ince was a hard-driving businessman. Over the previous decade he had almost single-handedly launched one of the film industry's most lucrative and enduring genres: the cowboy and Indian western. In large part because of Ince, generations of American children would watch wide-eyed as phony Apaches pounded on tom toms, heroes in ten-gallon hats made unlikely shots from horse-back, and the cavalry rode to the rescue. Ince missed his own birthday party because he was in Los Angeles feverishly negotiating a production deal—perhaps intended to finance one of his many westerns—with one of Hearst's investment companies. Once the deal was closed, however, Ince boarded a train and hurried down to San Diego to meet the *Oneida*.

A water taxi took Ince out to the yacht where, with the guest of honor finally aboard, the celebration proceeded in earnest. Actually, the celebrating was probably well advanced by the time Ince arrived. Although these were prohibition times, the *Oneida* was well stocked with champagne, and the guests Hearst had invited were people who knew how to enjoy themselves. These were the Roaring Twenties after all, and they roared more ferociously in California than in most places. By Sunday evening, people along the shore in San Diego could hear an audible roar rising through the portholes of the *Oneida*, where the partying reached a peak shortly after dinner. Then it turned a bit stale, for about that time something happened to Ince. To this day nobody knows for certain what it was, but within two days he was dead.

Later, the San Diego district attorney's office was told that, while on the *Oneida*, Ince was stricken with an acute bout of indigestion—probably he had eaten too much. Of course, no mention was made of the champagne. Nor was any mention made of the pearl-handled revolver Hearst kept in a drawer in his stateroom. The authorities were told that Ince had been rushed ashore with Dr. Daniel Goodman in attendance. A Hearst employee and non-practicing physician, Dr. Goodman happened to be on the *Oneida* when Ince fell ill. Dr. Goodman was said to have accompanied Ince by train to Los Angeles, where the producer grew even sicker. He died on November 19, supposedly of a heart attack, perhaps induced by his digestive condition. That, in any case, was the official version of events. Convinced that Ince had died of natural causes, the district attorney closed the book of his investigation with a resounding thump. It has never been reopened.

What really happened on the *Oneida* that Sunday in late November? Maybe events unfolded exactly as described by witnesses on the yacht, all of whom in one way or another were beholden to Hearst. But this seems unlikely, and even then most people didn't believe what increasingly sounded like a hastily patched together cover story. Some of Hearst's guests, Chaplin and Parsons among them, claimed never to have been onboard the *Oneida*. Chaplin had been away shooting a film and Parsons in New York working on a column. One of Hearst's newspapers even went so far as to place Ince in far off San Simeon rather than San Diego when he became "ill." Absurd denials and outright lies such as these were bound to start jaws flapping, and, indeed, the rumors flew. To some, it began to seem likely that Ince had been murdered, but if so, why and by whom? No one has ever satisfactorily answered these questions. Anyone who managed to answer them would resolve one of California's most fascinating mysteries.

A mystery is essentially a story or a series of stories layered one atop the other. Usually, the reader or observer gets to choose which of the stories best suits the available facts. Then the correct solution is revealed. The mystery associated with the death of Thomas Ince is like that, only in this case, the actual truth of the matter may never be known. It may even be that there is no one true solution. Readers may decide for themselves once they've examined the evidence, but unfortunately, there's not much. Mostly all we have is what we know about the various people involved in the incident. In addition to Ince, the main characters of our mystery are as follows.

CHARLIE CHAPLIN

One of the most innovative and influential film stars of all time, Charles Spencer Chaplin has always been closely associated with the Little Tramp, the silent film character he created. Everyone who has ever seen a Chaplin film—and hardly anyone on earth has not—is well acquainted with this awkward, but lovable figure. The Tramp has a good heart and always the best of intentions, but he gets into all sorts of difficulties and despite using a cane, has trouble standing up straight. Clumsy, ill at ease, and often downright silly, the Tramp is not the sort of fellow one would expect to see in the company of a beautiful young lady. However, the real Charlie Chaplin did not in the least resemble the character he played on film, especially when it came to his love relationships.

Chaplin was handsome, debonair, sure of himself, and enormously charming. He also, as they say, "had a way with women." Born in 1889 in London, Chaplin came to the United States shortly before World War I to work as a stage actor but before long had made himself a megastar of silent film. Chaplin's success and his work in film brought him into contact with some of the most attractive and eligible—or in some cases ineligible—women of the era. The list of Chaplin romances is impressive:

Hetta Kelly, a dancer and the object of a teenage infatuation; Edna Purviance, an actress and an early Chaplin leading lady; Mildred Harris, a sixteen-year-old child actress Chaplin married in 1918 and divorced two years later; Pola Negri, a Polish actress with whom Chaplin had a very public affair during the early 1920s; Louise Brooks, a Ziegfeld girl who had a fling with Chaplin in 1925; Lita Grey, another teenage actress wooed and married during the 1920s by Chaplin, who was more than twice her age; Merna Kennedy, a dancer who worked with Chaplin in his film *The Circus* and was said to have been the cause of his divorce from Lita Grey in 1927; Georgia Hale, a beautiful young actress with whom Chaplin maintained an intimate relationship during the late 1920s and early 1930s; May Reeves, Chaplin's secretary who had a brief 1930s affair with him, which ended when she became involved with his brother; Paulette Goddard, an actress who maintained a live-in relationship with Chaplin for nearly eight years during the 1930s; Joan Barry, a young actress who filed an unsuccessful paternity suit against Chaplin in 1943; and Oona O'Neill, the daughter of the famed playwright Eugene O'Neill and Chaplin's wife from 1943 until he died in 1977.

This substantial catalog of conquests is by no means the only evidence of the magnetic attraction Chaplin exerted on women—or of his virility. He was known to have had twelve children, eight of them with Oona. The last of his offspring, Christopher James Chaplin, was born in 1962 when Chaplin was seventy-three years old.

Left off the long list above is Marion Davies, but she was rumored to have had an on-and-off relationship with him from 1924 right on up into the 1930s. These may have been rumors only, and Hearst, Davies' longtime benefactor and companion, may or may not have had reasons to be jealous. Given Chaplin's reputation, however, Hearst would have been a blind fool not to have had suspicions of some sort, and of course, he was nobody's fool.

WILLIAM RANDOLPH HEARST

Born in San Francisco in 1863, Hearst was the son of a successful mining engineer. Hearst was still in his teens in 1880 when his father bought a controlling interest in the *San Francisco Examiner.* A few years later, after his graduation from Harvard, the young Hearst took over the *Examiner,* determined to make it the most popular and profitable newspaper in the West. Never particularly interested in mining, which had laid the foundation of his family's fortune, Hearst believed there were far richer veins of gold to be found in publishing than in the mountains of the West. Over the next six decades he feverishly worked those veins, building one of the most extensive publishing empires in the world and making so much money that, in time, even he had lost track of just how rich he had become.

Hearst's publishing success was based on his keen sense of what constituted news and upon his insistence on good writing. Hearst newspapers and magazines either hired or regularly published writers such as Mark Twain, Jack London, and Ambrose Bierce, who would become legends in their own times. However, Hearst's success was also based in part on what would come to be known as yellow journalism, a term that referenced the screaming yellow headlines that often bannered the front pages of Hearst newspapers.

Using techniques of this sort to influence public opinion, the Hearst newspaper chain could and, in more than one instance, did change the course of world history. A case in point is the Spanish American War, which without the "Remember the *Maine*" rabble-rousing promoted by Hearst and his editors, would likely never have happened. Apparently, Hearst did not care in the least whether Spanish authorities had or had not ordered the destruction of the U.S. battleship *Maine*. All that mattered to him was that war sold lots and lots of newspapers.

Eventually, Hearst became so rich and so powerful that he could live as he liked, and probably do anything he liked to anybody. No doubt Hearst understood this, but he seems to have been no more ruthless or licentious than most of the other business barons of his era. His most flamboyant excesses were poured into the bizarre mansion he built on top of a mountain at San Simeon, on California's central coast. Hearst made of it a rather nightmarish gallery of mismatched artwork he had purchased the world over. Hearst launched the San Simeon project in 1919 and, during the later years of his life, he retreated to his extravagant home there more and more often. His constant companion at San Simeon was Marion Davies.

MARION DAVIES

A fashion model and former Ziegfeld girl, Marion Davies began her acting career in 1917 at the age of twenty when she starred in *Runaway Romany,* a film directed by her brother-in-law, the well-known Broadway producer George Lederer. Davies starred in three more films the following year and soon became one of the most sought after screen actresses in America. People loved her large luminous eyes and childlike face. She was in demand, not just by producers and directors, but by men who craved her company and were anxious to be seen with her.

One of the men who wooed her was William Randolph Hearst. Apparently, she met him shortly before starring in the title role of *Celia and the Pink Roses,* a film backed by Hearst.

Among the most popular actresses of her era, sultry Marion Davies was said to be capable of exciting murderous passion in men.

Before long, she was at his side nearly all of the time, that is, when she was not making movies. By the time her film career ended in 1931, she had made several dozen of them. After 1931, she spent nearly all of her time with Hearst either at his San Simeon estate or at one of his other opulent homes. The fact that Hearst was married to another woman, the prominent socialite and philanthropist Millicent Hearst, never seemed to bother her. Hearst remained married to Millicent until he died in 1951, leaving half of his estate to Davies.

It would be easy to think of Davies as a sort of high-priced kept woman, but the truth is she had already earned a fortune as a screen personality before taking up with the tycoon, and she would earn more. When Hearst himself fell on hard financial times during the latter years of the Great Depression, she bailed him out with a check for $1 million, which she handed over, it is said, without so much as batting an eye. Apparently, her affection for Hearst was genuine and long lasting.

All of which brings us to the alleged affair between Davies and Chaplin. There can be little doubt that she could have and likely did catch Chaplin's eye, but did he catch hers? She would have met Chaplin at a very young and impressionable age, and Chaplin was certainly one to make an impression on a woman. When Chaplin stepped aboard the *Oneida* that Saturday in November 1924, was there already something going on between the Little Tramp and Marion Davies? And if so, did they betray their affections by saying or doing something that someone would have noticed? Someone, for instance, like William Randolph Hearst?

LOUELLA PARSONS

Said to have been on the guest list that Saturday was someone who almost certainly would have noticed if Chaplin and Davies had embraced or touched hands a little too warmly, or if Chaplin had appeared to whisper some sweet nothings in Davies's ear. That was the already notorious gossip columnist Louella Parsons. A journalist and later a radio broadcaster, Parsons reported on the doings of stars, starlets, and producers. She brought numerous scandals to the attention of a public endlessly fascinated by Hollywood and in the process wrecked many careers. It is difficult to imagine that had anything newsworthy—or unworthy—taken place aboard the *Oneida* she would not have reported it and used it to further her career. On the other hand, she worked for the *New York American,* a Hearst newspaper.

Ince died on the Tuesday following the celebration of his birthday. On Wednesday, the *Los Angeles Times*—not a Hearst newspaper—ran a brief, front-page, morning-edition story beneath a lurid headline: "Movie Producer Shot on Hearst Yacht." By the time the evening editions appeared on the streets, however, both the headline and the story had vanished. Either the *Times* editors realized they had the story wrong or someone had gotten to them.

If this was the beginning of a cover-up, it was soon in full swing. Hearst's own newspapers were soon reporting that Ince had been nowhere near the *Oneida* when he fell ill. Instead, he had been at the Hearst mansion in San Simeon. Whisked home in an ambulance, he had died of a heart attack, a fact supposedly attested to by the attending physician. Even though it soon became clear that Ince had been in San Diego at the time, and not in San Simeon, the Hearst papers never corrected the misstatement.

The cause of death was likewise an open question and will always remain so. Although the death certificate listed the official cause as heart failure, there was never any way to check its veracity. Ince's wife, Nell, refused requests for an autopsy and quickly had her husband's body cremated. Soon after his funeral, she boarded a plane and left for Europe. It may have been out of pure friendship and humanitarian concern that Hearst later established a sizable trust fund for Nell Ince and also paid off the mortgage on the posh Los Angeles apartment building the Inces had owned.

Although Ince had been one of the most important men in Hollywood, his funeral was not the major event that one might have expected. Largely ignored by the press, it was a rather quiet affair attended by family and a few friends. Among the latter was Charlie Chaplin, who nonetheless denied that he had been there and also denied that he had been with Hearst, Davies, Ince, and the others in San Diego. Parsons likewise denied having been there, and although she was one of the most prolific gossip mongers of the age, she never wrote a word about the incident. Why is that? All we know is that, soon after Ince's death, Hearst gave her an enhanced contract with more money and a wider syndication for her column. And what of Chaplin? He continued with his career and his various affairs as before, perhaps even meeting occasionally with Davies. His professional star burned brighter than ever, but then in the 1930s it began to fade a little. The Great Depression was on, and tramps and hobos no longer seemed quite so much a laughing matter.

So what really happened on that evening so long ago in San Diego? The most popular theory goes something like this. Chaplin and Davies were in fact having an affair and made this a bit too obvious to Hearst, who caught them in an embrace in the *Oneida* lounge. Flying into a jealous rage, Hearst then brandished a pistol and, either intentionally or accidentally, pulled the trigger. If he had intended to hit Chaplin, however, he missed. Instead, the bullet struck Ince, who most unfortunately for him, was just then stepping into the lounge. Since the shooting was more or less an accident and not knowing whether or not Ince would survive, the principles decided that it would be best for all concerned if the incident were permanently hushed up.

There are, of course, many other theories. One of these holds that Davies and Ince were having a friendly conversation in the *Oneida* galley. In a murderous frame of mind, Hearst walked in on them, and mistaking Ince for Chaplin, pulled a gun and fired. Yet another theory leaves Hearst out of the equation altogether and perhaps Chaplin and Davies as well. It is said two other passengers were having a furious argument in one of the staterooms, and one of them pulled a pistol. While the adversaries struggled for possession of the weapon, it accidentally discharged. The bullet then passed through the thin wooden walls into another cabin where it struck the once again very unlucky Mr. Ince.

Adding credence to the various pistol theories is the eyewitness account of one Toraichi Kono, a Japanese immigrant who served as Chaplin's personal secretary. A keen observer of fact, Kono told friends that he had noticed a serious head wound when Ince was carried from the yacht. Oddly enough, Kono was never interviewed by the police or by the district attorney.

On the other hand, Ince may have died, as the official record maintains, of complications resulting from a simple case of indigestion. He would not have been the first to have passed into the great beyond after eating a bad oyster or ingesting far too much champagne and caviar. Sometimes the most banal explanations are the best, and not every mystery has a guilty party.

You can decide for yourself whether this particular mystery has a culprit or a plausible solution, or you can let the Hollywood folks themselves decide for you. Released in 2002, the movie *Cat's Meow,* directed by Peter Bogdanovich, attempts to unravel the whole tangled web. Starring Edward Herrmann as William Randolph Hearst, Eddie Izzard as Charlie Chaplin, Kirsten Dunst as Marion Davies, Cary Elwes as Thomas Ince, and Jennifer Tilly as Louella Parsons, *Cat's Meow* may or may not be historically accurate, but it is well worth a look. This book will not spoil the fun by revealing the ending.

So was William Randolph Hearst a murderer? Before making up your mind, consider that crime—even murder—takes many forms not all of which can be brought before a judge and jury. Decades before he bought his yacht or took up with Marion Davies, Hearst had ordered his biggest dailies to push for war with Spain even though he knew the causes for war were spurious at best. Urged to action by Hearst's great yellow headlines, Congress declared war. This resulted in the slaughter of thousands of American and Spanish soldiers and sailors, not to mention thousands of innocent civilians all of whom died, it would seem, in order to help Hearst and others sell morning editions. It may be worth noting that there are newspaper and cable television tycoons today who behave as Mr. Hearst behaved. The mystery and the tragedy inherent in this is that none dare accuse them of anything more sinister than greed.

CHAPTER 5

Where Is the Head of Zorro?

The corrupt officials, thieving tax collectors, and mercilessly greedy landlords of early nineteenth-century California would have been well advised to steer clear of dark corners, dim hallways, or unlighted streets. One could never be sure that Zorro, the Fox, was not lurking there somewhere in the shadows, and as everyone knows, he was no friend of villains. Zorro wore dark clothing and a black hat, cape, and mask, the better to slink unseen and unrecognized through the gloom. The night was Zorro's native element and his refuge, and whenever he stepped briefly into the light, it was nearly always with sword in hand. He used his blade with almost superhuman skill in order to right wrongs and, like Robin Hood, steal from the rich and give to the poor. Then, no sooner had he relieved some fat scoundrel of an even fatter purse than he leapt onto his faithful steed and rode off into the hills not to be seen again until he next returned to strike a blow for the poor and the powerless.

Never very bright, nimble, or competent, the soldiers mustered by unscrupulous Spanish authorities could never catch Zorro and the musket balls and pistol slugs they fired after him never came close. If they pushed into the mountains to seek out his lair, they had no chance of finding him for he had not merely gone into hiding—he had vanished altogether. During the day, Zorro traded in his cape and mask for the trappings of a dandy, a well-respected and immaculately dressed Spanish nobleman by the name of Don Diego de la Vega. Rather shy and notoriously clumsy with a sword, Don Diego was averse to violence and not particularly interested in the senoritas—something that could not be said of his nocturnal alter ego. How could anyone ever suspect such a wimpy fellow of harboring a hero complex? No one ever did, and Zorro kept showing up night after night to perform feats of derring-do and leave his trademark "Z" carved on the walls of presidios or on the carriage doors of the rich.

Such is the legend of El Zorro, one of the most celebrated figures of the West and of Old California. The caped horseman has found his way into countless short stories, novels, picture books, comic strips, theater cliff-hangers, serialized television dramas, and feature-length Hollywood movies. Among the dozens of actors who have portrayed him on screen are Douglas Fairbanks, Robert Livingston, Reed Hadley, Tyrone Power, Guy Williams, Anthony Hopkins, and Antonio Banderas, who played Zorro's successor in a pair of more recent film revivals.

Most of the story of Zorro is pure myth, unsupported by historical facts of any sort, but there is a kernel of truth in the legend. During the Gold Rush era, a bold young bandit haunted the hills of Central and Southern California and on occasion charged through its dry valleys on horseback in search of gold and plunder. It is not at all clear that he was, as many believe, a sort of western Robin Hood, but his life and death became the stuff of legend. His name was Joaquin Murrieta.

Very little is known for certain about Murrieta, and the verifiable facts concerning him are so few that his life story is almost as much a fiction as that of Zorro. For instance, some say Murrieta was born about 1829 in the town of Alamos in northwestern Mexico, while others say he was actually born much earlier than that in Chile. Like so many thousands of other hopeful forty-niners, he is believed to have migrated to California to prospect for gold. He is said to have found it, too, on a hillside or along a stream somewhere in the California Sierra, but he was not allowed to cash in on his strike.

According to one of the many stories associated with Murrieta, a group of Anglo miners attacked him and stole his gold, leaving him seriously wounded. They also beat and raped his wife. This violent and tragic incident is said to have transformed Murrieta from a hardworking miner into a bandit and social revolutionary. From this time forward, he no longer attempted to make his fortune by scraping it one nugget at a time from the earth, but instead took gold, money, and valuables from any Anglo miner or rancher he happened across.

During the early 1850s Murrieta formed a band of outlaws, five of whom coincidentally had the same first name. In addition to Murrieta, his gang included Joaquin Botellier, Joaquin Carrillo, Joaquin Ocomorenia, and Joaquin Valenzuela, a circumstance that may have led to considerable confusion whenever the bandits addressed one another. For obvious reasons, the gang soon came to be called the "Five Joaquins." The only key member of the gang not named Joaquin was Manuel Garcia, better known to both his victims and associates as "Three Fingered Jack" because, after years of gun fighting and swordplay, that is the number of fingers he still possessed. Burning ranches, rustling cattle and horses, plundering supply wagons, and sacking small towns and mining camps, Murrieta and his associates became the scourge of the Sierras and of the California Valley. Meanwhile, the activities of the Joaquins and their three-fingered friend understandably attracted the attention of California authorities.

A full-time company of California Rangers was organized to hunt down the bandits, and a reward of up to $1,000 was placed—quite literally—on Murrieta's head. In command of the rangers was Harry Love, a lawman and soldier of fortune who, just like Murrieta, had drifted to California hoping to strike it rich. Not much of a miner, he found no gold or silver and was soon offering his services as a bounty hunter. Murrieta represented a very big prize indeed for Love, for the bounty was soon upped to $5,000. Governor John Bigler, at that time in office for little more than a year, was willing to spend whatever it took to rein in the Joaquins. Bigler understood only too well that, if he failed, the voters would want his head as well as Murrieta's, so he saw to it that Love's rangers were well equipped and well paid. They each received $150 per month, a handsome salary at a time when many workers made little more than that for a full year of hard labor. On three separate occasions Love's Rangers thought they had the bandits cornered, but Murrieta and his men always managed to slip away into the mountains. Then came the afternoon of July 25, 1853. Near the summit of Pacheco Pass in San Benito County about fifty miles southeast of Monterey, Love and about twenty of his rangers came upon a group of Mexicans camped under a tree. The rangers asked no questions, pistols were drawn, and there ensued a very brief and deadly shootout. The Mexicans got by far the worst of it, and when the shooting was over, two of them were dead. One was believed to be Murrieta and the other Three Fingered Jack.

To prove that they had been successful and make sure they could claim the governor's reward, the rangers cut off the head of the man believed to be Murrieta and the mostly fingerless hand of his companion. This gruesome evidence was preserved in a barrel of brandy and taken to the new state capitol in Sacramento. Love then received his reward, some of which he parceled out to the other rangers.

Love invested his reward in a ranch just outside of Santa Cruz. However, he was not much better at ranching than he had been at prospecting and soon went broke. Some would say he was cursed, for a seemingly endless series of fires, floods, and other calamities dogged him wherever he went. Finally, ruined, penniless, and severely depressed, he moved onto the property of his estranged wife, Mary, near Santa Clara. In 1868 he was killed in a scuffle with the bodyguard Mary Love had hired to protect her from her increasingly unstable and violent husband.

By this time Love had been largely forgotten by his fellow Californians, but not so Murrieta. Having been identified by a priest and at least sixteen other people who had met the bandit or had known him personally, Murrieta's head was stuffed into a large pickle jar filled with preservative. The jar was then put on display in Mariposa, Stockton, San Francisco, and elsewhere, and people were charged $1 each just to see it. Thousands of people were willing to pay this high price—more than a day's wage for many—to examine the jar because they knew they were gazing upon a legend.

No sooner had Murrieta been killed than the stories told concerning him began to multiply and grow ever more romantic. Some of these were collected into a series of San Francisco newspaper articles written by John Rollin Ridge, a Cherokee Indian. Published in 1854—only a year after the bandit died—these fictionalized accounts made of Murrieta a tragic hero. Attacked in the Sierra by Gringo thugs, he had been forced to watch as his brother was hanged and his beloved young wife was raped and killed. Then he himself was bullwhipped to the point of unconsciousness and left to die. Unfortunately for his attackers, Murrieta survived, and filled with a fierce desire for revenge, he hunted them down one by one and punished their crimes with pistol and sword. When all were dead, he continued his crusade by stealing from wealthy Yanquis and sharing the loot with impoverished Spanish-speaking settlers. Not surprisingly, perhaps, Ridge claimed Murrieta was not entirely of Mexican heritage—he was part Cherokee. Some of what Ridge had written may have had a slim basis in fact, but Murrieta was almost certainly not a Cherokee.

Ridge was not the only one to claim some link, whether racial or otherwise, with the famous bandit. Practically every town and village in the state had residents who swore that Murrieta had put in an appearance there. For instance, there were those in Stockton who claimed to have noticed an impressive young Mexican ride into town one Sunday morning in 1852. Wearing a tall sombrero, silver belt buckle, and other finery, he graciously greeted everyone he met along the town's main street. At the post office, he spent a long while staring at a poster offering $5,000 for the capture of Murrieta. Then the young man wrote something on the poster, mounted his well-groomed black horse, and rode away. Afterward, someone noticed that the figure $5,000 had been scratched out and the sum $10,000 written over it. Beside this was signed the name "Joaquin."

Although the Murrieta legend fascinated nearly all Californians, it was especially dear to those of Mexican heritage. Murrieta had given them a Latin hero, one who had fought back against oppressive Gringo land-grabbers and resisted the flood tide of Anglo culture. There were even those among them who refused to believe that Murrieta was dead. They were certain that at Pacheco Pass the rangers had killed and mutilated two innocent Mexican ranch hands so they could claim the reward money. Murrieta himself was still up there in the mountains somewhere prepared to ride to the rescue whenever his people needed him.

One day in 1854 a young woman paid her dollar and had a look at the pickle jar supposedly containing Murrieta's head. She said she was Murrieta's sister and that the head in the jar was definitely not his. No one would ever know for certain whether she was telling the truth. Though many people claimed to have seen him alive and well many years after Pacheco Pass, no one could ever prove it. The only evidence that remained was the head itself which ended up behind the bar in the Golden Nugget Saloon in San Francisco. Some said the head was destroyed by the inferno that consumed the bar along with much of the city following the Great San Francisco Earthquake of 1906, but by that time there were few who cared whether or not it had ever been attached to the body of Joaquin Murrieta.

Murrieta's admirers were quite correct to maintain that he was not dead. He had merely taken refuge in a new and more shadowy realm: the world of fiction. Over the years, he had acquired a black mask, cape, and flat-brimmed gaucho hat. He also received a new moniker when, in the early decades of the twentieth century, he began to be called El Zorro after the Spanish word for fox. That is the title pulp-fiction writer Johnston McCulley gave him in *The Curse of Capistrano,* a story featured in a 1919 edition of the adventure fiction magazine *All-Story Weekly,* which later became *Argosy.* The caped swordsman proved an instant success, and thereafter Zorro became the almost exclusive focus of McCulley's writing career. Over the next forty years, McCulley wrote no fewer than sixty-five Zorro books and short stories attracting up to five hundred million readers worldwide with translations into more than two dozen languages.

Zorro was also a hit at the box office. The ink was barely dry on the *All-Story Weekly's Curse* edition when Douglas Fairbanks signed to play the hero of the 1920 silent-film blockbuster *The Mark of Zorro.* Five years later Fairbanks rode back onto the screen all dressed in black for a sequel, *Don Q, Son of Zorro.* Many more films and television treatments were to follow.

During the 1950s, when Walt Disney announced his intention to produce the television series *Zorro* for ABC, everyone knew it would be a big winner. Consequently, dozens of actors, including Dennis Weaver, David Janssen, Jack Kelley, and John Lupton tried out for the title role, but it was Guy Williams who landed the part. A New Yorker whose real name was Armando Catalano, Williams had a Spanish heritage, and this may have given him the edge. Williams brought an air of European sophistication to his portrayal of the aristocratic Don Diego, as well as a thrilling athleticism to Zorro. Gene Sheldon took the role of Diego's mute—verbally challenged—sidekick, played with a humor that might not be tolerated by today's politically correct audiences. Henry Calvin played the bumbling Sergeant Garcia and George Lewis played Don Alejandro, Don Diego's father, with a grace befitting a Castilian gentleman. The overall effect was delightful and, although the series ran for only two years, unforgettable. Although highly entertaining, it left a patently false impression of what life was like in early California.

Today, Zorro ranks among the best-loved and most widely known fictional characters of all time. Brought to life in prose and on screen for half a dozen generations, he has popularized an otherwise little-known period of Mexican, American, and California history: the era of the rancheros. Zorro supposedly rode through the night at a time when a few hundred powerful landowners such as Don Alejandro ran enormous herds of cattle through the grassy California vales, regularly exchanging their hides for heaps of gold and silver coin. Murrieta, on the other hand, had started out as a hardworking miner during the Gold Rush, which put an emphatic end to the ranchero way of life. The only dealings Murrieta had with cattle were when he rustled them.

The story of Murrieta was to take yet another very long step off the path of historical truth. During the 1930s, a cartoonist by the name of Bob Kane created a masked and caped character, one who led a dual life, performed astounding feats of athleticism, and popped up as if from thin air whenever there were wrongs in need of correction. Basing his dark crusader almost entirely on the silent-movie version of Zorro—he was a big fan of Douglas Fairbanks—Kane called him Batman. Since then, publishers and producers have cranked out endless Batman stories, an activity they consider an acceptable alternative to actually printing money. And so it happened that a poor Mexican miner who turned to banditry and whose head has gone missing now for more than a century was destined to become one of the world's favorite fantasy figures. In a sense, this is no mystery for we all need heroes whether masked or otherwise.

CHAPTER 6

Ships Afloat on Sand and Fog

C harley Clusker literally could not believe what he was seeing. He was tired, hungry, and thirsty—oh, so thirsty—and the blazing orb of the desert sun had seared his eyes day after day for more than a week. He was half blind, maybe more than half, and he knew it. He was so exhausted that he could only be certain that his name was Charley and perhaps not even of that. If someone had told him right then and there that he was President Ulysses S. Grant, he might have believed it, but not this, not a ship run aground in the middle of the California Desert. Yet, there it was, its hull and masts rising from the rolling dunes about a half mile up ahead.

Charley knew perfectly well what this was all about. He was a grizzled, Gold Rush prospector who regularly plunged into the wilderness with a donkey, a pan, and a few days' worth of sourdough. He had arrived too late in California to stake a worthwhile claim in the Sierra. All the rich veins there were now owned and jealously guarded by others, and many of the best

Sierra mines had long since played out. So Charley had turned to the desert where he fully expected to find gold, silver, or at least something of great value. Having attained and passed the age of sixty, he had not yet struck it rich and made his fortune, but he had learned a few things during his years of prospecting. For instance, he knew all about mirages and how a person's eyes will lie to them in the shimmering, midday desert heat. That's what this was, he thought—a mirage and a lie.

However, this mirage was different from any of the others he had seen. Unlike most mirages, it didn't dance like an imp along the horizon, and it didn't constantly retreat, seeming always out of reach. The fact was, he was gaining on this thing, and its outlines were growing more and more distinct all the time. What had started out as a tiny, dark spot set against a background of sun-bleached rock and sand had steadily increased in size, becoming ever more substantial and undeniably real, until there he was standing before it, unable to believe, but equally unable to deny. It is easy to imagine that, at this point, Charley's tired and shaky legs could no longer hold him and that he fell to his knees and either laughed or cried.

It was a ship all right, lying there half-buried in the sand. It was big, too, larger than any manmade structure Charley had ever seen in the open desert. Its bow and stern stood more than 100 feet apart, but for all its size, it seemed to be losing its battle with the dunes—perhaps it had already lost long ago. The fierce winds had broken its masts, and Charley could see one of them

Thanks to photographer Tomas Castelazo

From a distance, a jumble of desert rocks and cactus like this one may appear to be the hull and masts of an old ship that seems to have sailed miraculously far off course. The heat and glare of the midday sun can heighten the illusion.

sticking out of the sand a short distance from the hull. On one side the ship's gunnels rose only a few inches out of the sand and on the other not at all. The bone dry desert air had so shrunk the planking that one could see clear through the hull as if it were the desiccated chest cavity of a dead horse. No, this hull would never float upon a river, a lake, or the sea again. If this land were covered with water instead of sand and gravel, the old ship would surely be on the bottom.

Peering through the openings in the hull, Charley could see chests. Perhaps they contained gold, silver, pearls, or precious jewels. Charley had heard stories of a Spanish treasure ship that had sailed up the flooded Colorado River and gotten stuck somewhere far to the west of where the river flows today. Perhaps this was it. Unfortunately, Charley was too tired and too near death from thirst to break through the planking and find out what those chests contained. So he pushed on searching for something that at the moment seemed far more valuable to him than gold or pearls—water.

Charley Clusker told a story something like the one above when he wandered out of the desert and into the hardscrabble town of Indio at the head of the Imperial Valley sometime during the fall of 1870. He repeated his fantastic account to general store owners, corral operators, assay office clerks, bartenders, and even bankers—anyone he felt might have the slightest inclination to set him up with a grubstake. He needed the stake so he could go out into the desert, find the ship again, and then bring back all that treasure. No doubt, most who heard Charley's story were not prepared to accept a word of it as truth, but when quick and easy fortunes are promised, there is always someone willing to believe. Before long, Charley had scraped together enough money for the necessary equipment and sourdough and, perhaps, a fresh donkey or mule.

One in Indio who did believe Charley or said he did was a correspondent for the *Los Angeles Star*. The *Star* operated in a highly competitive environment and was not overly particular about the veracity of the stories it printed, so long as they sold newspapers. Based on Charley's report and others and, in some instances, likely based on nothing at all, the *Star* regaled its readers with lurid tales of Spanish galleons that had become lost at the head the Gulf of California and had somehow been swept inland, of pirate ships that had run aground in a backwater of the Colorado River, and even of an ancient warship sent to America by Israel's King Solomon which, by navigational means that defy the imagination, ended up in the deserts of the American Southwest.

All of these inventive scenarios concerning the origins of Charley's lost ship had in common one highly speculative theory, namely that the Gulf of California and thus the Pacific Ocean had once been linked to the Imperial Valley's Salton Sinks by way of a narrow passage. The sinks are, in fact, below sea level, and it is not inconceivable that they were once connected to the Pacific. However, geologists assure us that this link, if it ever existed at all, was permanently closed and walled off from the ocean, not hundreds or even thousands, but millions of years ago. Of course, none of this was understood back in 1870, and if it had been, the *Star*'s fiction-loving editors would not have cared.

In its November 12, 1870, edition, the *Star* reported that Charley had found the investors he needed and was headed back out into the desert to search for his lost treasure ship. "Charley Clusker started out again this morning," said the *Star,* giving as his intended destination a stretch of sandy waste near the tiny village of Dos Palmas. "He is well prepared with a good wagon, pack saddles, and planks to cross the sandy ground."

Despite his careful preparations, apparently funded by several of Indio's more gullible businessmen, Charley returned having found nothing. Though brief, the trip had nearly cost him his life. "He was without food or water, under a hot broiling sun for over twenty-four hours, and came near perishing," said the *Star*.

The editors speculated that perhaps Charley would not try again, but he did, this time in the company of other prospectors who had signed on the expedition as junior partners. By December Charley and company were back in Indio and their return was ballyhooed in the *Star*. "Charley Clusker and party returned from the desert yesterday, just as we were going to press," said the wildly enthusiastic report. "They had a hard time of it, but they have succeeded in their effort. The ship has been found!"

Interestingly enough, the report did not mention that any gold, pearls, or other valuables had been brought back from the wreck. It seems the prospectors had returned empty-handed. In an optimistic postscript, the *Star* mentioned that "Charley returns to the desert today, to reap the fruition of his labors."

That was the last anyone saw or heard of Charley. At least, it was the last time his name was ever mentioned in the *Star*. It would appear that, like the crew of the Colorado Desert's lost ship and the identity of their vessel, Charley Clusker had vanished into the trackless wastes of history. The ghost ship he had sought, however, would not be forgotten.

For at least two centuries before the stories about Charley and his lost ship appeared in the *Los Angeles Star,* people had reported seeing something strange in the deserts to the west of the Colorado River. Early eighteenth-century Spanish explorers said they had seen something that looked like a ship out there. The Indians said they had seen it, too. So did early wagon-train immigrants who took the less mountainous southern route into California. What was it? Whatever it was, old desert rats and prospectors like Charley Clusker and travelers willing to take the risk of crossing the waterless Mojave and Colorado Deserts kept seeing it and reporting their sightings once they had reached more civilized places. During the 1890s, three German prospectors said they had seen the ship, and they actually brought back pieces of wood said to have been torn from its planking. In 1933, a naturalist out sketching desert wildflowers reported the discovery of what was believed to be a Viking long ship in a deep arroyo. Before anyone could investigate, the arroyo was said to have been buried in a landslide caused by an earthquake.

Why do people believe they've seen ships in the desert? An easy explanation may be that, affected by the heat and the monotony of the landscape, they may see a long pointed rock or knoll and imagine that it is the hull of a large, seagoing vessel. The desert air can bend light in odd ways, and from a distance, a Joshua tree or saguaro cactus can look very much like the masts of an old sailing ship. There are many, however, who are not satisfied with answers of this sort.

Some say the idea that a ship could have become stranded in the desert is perfectly logical and believable. They point out that the lower reaches of the Colorado River were once navigable and that it is prone to extensive floods capable of spilling over into the desert. As proof of this they point to the 1905 flood that not only poured into the desert but actually broke through a series of manmade irrigation canals into the Imperial Valley, forming what is now referred to as the Salton Sea. It was believed at the time that the inundated portions of the valley would soon dry up and return to their original parched condition, but this never happened. The thirty-mile-long brackish water lake remains as a testament to the power and unpredictable nature of the Earth. So, if Colorado River floodwaters could form a small sea in one of the hottest, driest places on Earth, why couldn't they carry a ship there?

According to a narrative assembled by a historical novelist by the name of Antonio de Fierro Blanco, just such a thing actually happened during the early seventeenth century. Obsessed with the trappings of great wealth, King Phillip III of Spain is said to have sent an expedition to America to search for pearls. Having worked the rich oyster beds at the north end of the Gulf of California, a Spanish ship and crew under the command of Juan de Iturbe sailed into the mouth of the Colorado to look for more. As it turned out, the river was in flood at the time, and

Iturbe took his vessel into what appeared to be a vast bay. He even thought he might have discovered the long sought Strait of Anion said to link the waters of the Pacific with those of the Atlantic. Unfortunately for Iturbe and his crew, he had not. His ship got stuck in a muddy backwater and could not be freed. Soon, the waters of what Iturbe had hoped was a permanent ocean strait drained away back toward the Colorado, leaving his ensnared ship high and dry. The Spaniards were forced to abandon their vessel along with an enormous fortune in pearls and march through the desert to the shores of the gulf where they were eventually rescued. If any of this is true, then the remains of a Spanish galleon may indeed be buried in California's desert sands along with, perhaps, a chest or two of very fine old pearls.

YANKEE BLADE

The ocean is a kind of desert, and just as the salty sands of southeastern California may hide ruined Spanish treasure galleons, so may the salt waters of the state's Pacific coast cover sunken windjammers and steamships filled with bullion. As a matter of fact, those who search for treasure-laden wrecks might do better to turn their attentions from the desert to Point Arguello about three hundred miles south of San Francisco and 150 miles northwest of Los Angeles. Somewhere out there in the ocean about a mile off the point lie the remains of the *Yankee Blade*, a passenger steamer that came to grief on a relatively calm night in the autumn of 1854. Down with her this unfortunate vessel took a considerable number of prospectors who had gotten rich in the goldfields but never lived to enjoy their newfound wealth. Also lost was a huge shipment of gold estimated to have been worth more than $150,000 at the time and incalculably more today. Some, though not all, of the gold was recovered. The rest remains in the ocean, perhaps scattered along the bottom among the rocks, mussels, and oysters.

There is a bit of mystery about what happened to the *Yankee Blade*. She was not lost in a storm. Nor was she the victim of an uncharted reef. Instead, her captain apparently sailed her straight up onto the rocks just offshore. How or why did this happen?

The tragic truth of the matter is that accidents of this sort have happened frequently along this particular stretch of coast. Point Arguello is located a dozen miles or so north of Point Conception where the mostly southward-trending coast of California takes a sudden turn toward the east and the city of Los Angeles. Unless they wait until they have passed Point Conception before changing course and steering eastward, navigators of vessels bound for the City of Angels will end up among the angels along with their passengers and crew. That is apparently what happened to the *Yankee Blade*.

Launched in 1853 in New York, the *Yankee Blade* was a 275-foot side-wheel steamer displacing 1,767 tons. Having served for a few months on the East Coast, she was purchased by Cornelius Vanderbilt and dispatched by way of Cape Horn to California. There she was expected to increase the tycoon's already sizable fortune by providing reliable steam-powered passenger service to those who could afford it—namely California businessmen and miners who had struck it rich in the goldfields.

On September 30, 1854, the steamer took on 822 passengers and more than a ton of gold bullion. Counting the captain and crew, there were nearly a thousand people onboard when the ship set sail that same afternoon from San Francisco. Steaming safely out through the Golden Gate, the vessel turned south toward Panama, a destination she was not fated to reach.

With the weather favorable and her big steam engines churning, the voyage went well for more than a day. Then the *Yankee Blade*'s master ordered her to turn into the Santa Barbara Channel. Perhaps deceived by fog or haze, the captain thought he had cleared Point Conception. Unfortunately, he had not, and by the time his mistake became apparent, it was too late. With a sickening lurch, the *Yankee Blade* struck the rocks about three hundred yards off Point Arguello and stuck fast.

Her hull fatally punctured, the ship began to sink while her passengers fought one another for places in the lifeboats. There were not nearly enough of them—as would be the case many years later when the *Titanic* had her fatal encounter with a North Atlantic iceberg. Many people fell overboard and were drowned or crushed in the pounding surf. Many had filled their pockets with gold, and the heavy metal dragged them down to their deaths. Others discarded their valuables and even their clothing in hopes of saving themselves by swimming ashore. Most who tried to swim never made it.

Fewer than half of those onboard would reach land, but even there they were not safe. Hearing of the wreck, merciless bandits descended on Point Arguello to rob and terrorize the survivors. Some were murdered by these ruthless thieves before a unit of the California National Guard finally came to the rescue.

The wreck of the *Yankee Blade* was one of the worst disasters of the Gold Rush era. Nearly as many lives were lost—more than four hundred—as were killed in California during the entire war with Mexico. Since nobody knows how much money, gold, and other valuables the victims had with them, it is impossible to accurately estimate the financial losses—or to say how much treasure might still be out there in the ocean. To this day, people walk the cliffs and rock-strewn beaches of Point Arguello hoping to find a broken piece of the *Yankee Blade*'s shattered hull or even a gold nugget or two. When the fog rolls in, as it does nearly every day, they may glance occasionally toward the west, for it is said the ship itself can sometimes be seen floating in the air just off shore like the fabled *Flying Dutchman*.

CHAPTER 7

People Who Eat People

A particularly nasty myth associated with California is that people here are prone to eat each other. From a technical point of view, at least, this is not really true. Californians are known to appreciate hamburgers, hot dogs, pickle relish, processed cheese, chocolate candy, ice cream, and lots of the other stuff that Americans elsewhere eat. People in the Golden State do consume some rather strange stuff sometimes, but this has far more to do with current diet fads than with a shortage of meat. Californians largely observe the nearly universal taboo against eating human flesh, although it may be worth noting that the state has no law against doing so. Even so, there has not been a single documented case of cannibalism in California for more than 160 years. Go back before the days of the Gold Rush, however, and you encounter at least one very notorious instance.

A gruesome series of events unfolded on the eastern slopes of the California Sierra during the unusually cold and snowy winter of 1846–1847. There a small wagon train of

California-bound pioneers became trapped by deep snowdrifts that had piled up in the mountain passes, and as weeks wore into months, they ran desperately short of supplies. Inevitably, they began to starve. What they did to relieve their starvation would make of their experience one of the most widely discussed and horrific legends of the West. These unfortunate wayfarers, a once hopeful group of several dozen eastern farmers and their families, will forever be remembered as the Donner Party.

Winter lingers in the Sierras where the snows often do not melt until people elsewhere are enjoying summer. So by March 27, 1847, when George Donner drew his last breaths, these rugged mountains were still a cold and terribly unfriendly place. Weakened and perhaps delirious from hunger and exposure, Donner may yet have possessed the mental energy to think back over the trials he had faced along with his family and friends and the awful things he had seen. He had witnessed people and oxen with their tongues parched to leather by thirst on the trackless salt flats of Great Basin. He had witnessed murder and been forced to banish a close friend—the accused murderer—from his camp, consigning him to almost certain death in the wilderness. He had struggled up the nearly vertical Sierra passes only to see his hope of reaching safety in the California heartland slam head-on into an early winter blizzard. He had watched as members of the emigrant party that would forever after bear his family name died off one by one, the victims of starvation, illness, and cold. Some say he had also seen friends consume the dead bodies of other friends. According to legend, he may even have eaten human flesh himself. Now he was dying and almost certainly his wife and remaining family would soon follow him in death.

Like most stories, the one associated with Donner and his companions started long before reaching its climax—in this case an especially grisly one. Its roots lay in the waves of immigration that started moving westward in the early 1840s. It's hard to say what got the wheels of the first great wagon trains turning. Perhaps it was hard times and joblessness or the threat of cholera in the cities or the disappearance of cheap land in the East. More likely, however, it was the reawakening of a golden dream that had driven Americans westward since colonial times—the notion that out there somewhere a better life awaited them.

In the spring of 1846, that peculiarly American wanderlust burned in the hearts of George Donner and James Reed, who, along with more than twenty other members of their extended families, packed up their belongings, bid farewell to friends, and set out for California. Donner was a prosperous Illinois farmer and Reed a successful Springfield businessman, so these were no desperate people in need of a change of fortune. Their reasons for joining the thousands of other pioneers who set off into the wilderness that year were more personal than financial. Donner had already moved five times before settling in Illinois, so he was something of a rolling stone. Now he craved one more great adventure. Reed, whose restless intelligence had helped earn him a small fortune, hoped to prove himself anew in the West.

In the beginning the Donner Party numbered thirty-two, counting wives, children, and various relatives, and half a dozen or so hired hands and teamsters who were needed to drive the nine heavy wagons. Among the latter was Reed's extra-large family wagon, a veritable house on wheels. The Reeds called it their "pioneer palace car." A two-story contraption equipped with bunks and a built-in iron stove, it was to break the hearts of more than a few of the oxen that struggled to pull it. Despite the heft of their wagons, which other pioneers along the way considered extravagant, the party reached Independence, Missouri, without any serious incident.

Most western-bound migrants rested their animals at Independence and gathered themselves for the long, hard journey ahead. Between Independence and the Pacific lay three mighty mountain ranges, a series of scorching deserts, and more than two thousand miles of wilderness. The crossing could be accomplished, as more than half a million Americans would eventually prove, but it was not something to be undertaken lightly. For one thing, the entire trip had to be completed in just six months. Travelers could not start out from Missouri until the mud on the high plains left behind by the spring rains began to dry out. Then, they had to reach their destination before the first winter blizzards swept over the Sierras and blocked the passes with snow.

Leaving Independence on May 12, the Donners and Reeds were neither the first nor the last of the 1846 pioneers to crack their whips and launch themselves into the great western ocean of grass and sage. In the beginning they made good time but inevitably, there were delays caused by broken wheels, tired animals, sick children, or violent prairie storms. It was frustrating, and as they rattled along through wagon ruts so deep that many remain to this day, Donner and Reed began to wonder if there might be some way to make up for lost time.

Most wagons heading west that year, as in other years, followed a heavily beaten path that arched north of the Wasatch Mountains and the Great Salt Lake all the way to the foothills of the Sierras. But George Donner had in his possession a book entitled *Emigrant's Guide to Oregon and California* in which the author, one Lansford Hastings, recommended a shortcut. Rather than go around the rugged Wasatch Range, the new route plunged into it and, once clear of the mountains, crossed the utterly barren and waterless flats to the south of the Great Salt Lake. Despite the apparent difficulties, it would, Hastings claimed, lop several hundred miles off the trip. For days on end Donner and Reed debated the notion of taking a chance on the new Hastings route. Finally, despite dire warnings from trappers and mountain men they met along the way, they decided to chance it.

On July 18 the wagons rumbled across the Continental Divide, which nearly every western traveler considered the point of no return. Two days later they reached the Little Sandy River, where they parted ways with most of the other wagons headed for California. Turning south toward Fort Bridger and away from the main trail, the nine Donner and Reed wagons were accompanied by about twenty others owned by fellow migrants who likewise hoped to save time by taking the so-called Hastings Cut. The Donner Party of legend had formed.

Soon after they left the Little Sandy, the heads of the various families met—and though James Reed might have been a more logical choice—selected George Donner as their leader. Few thought Donner would lead for very long anyway, since they expected to meet up with none other than Lansford Hastings himself at Fort Bridger just a few days up ahead. They had heard that Hastings was waiting there to show travelers the way through his cut.

What no one in the Donner Party even suspected, however, was that Hastings knew very little about the supposed shortcut he had so glowingly described in his book. He had not explored it and was actually seeing it for the very first time that year. Hastings was what we would call these days a "fast-talking promoter." Having visited California a few years earlier, he was determined to place himself at the center of a political and commercial empire in the West, and to do that he needed to populate the region as fast as possible. Hastings thought his new shortcut might serve that purpose. Instead, it proved a disaster for more than a few unwary migrants who wandered into it and became ensnared like a fly in a spider's web. Among those who became trapped in this way was the Donner Party.

By the time Donner, Reed, and the others reached Fort Bridger on July 31, Hastings had already left at the head of another small convoy of wagons. George Donner urged on the members of his party in an effort to catch up to Hastings, but to no avail. Deeper and deeper they descended into the tangle of canyons, dry washes, and scrubby plains that lay before them, but try as they might, they could not catch Hastings. Meanwhile, precious time evaporated as the Donner Party crawled along, felling large trees and dragging aside boulders that stood in their way. Often they covered little more than two miles a day, and as they creaked along through the Wasatch and across the Great Basin, autumn with its mountain blizzards, marched inexorably toward them.

The seemingly endless white salt flats beyond the shores of the Great Salt Lake nearly destroyed the party. Hastings had written that this eighty-mile-wide desert could be crossed in "two days of hard driving." Instead, the crossing took five days, and by the time the wagons reached the other side, many of the party's precious oxen had died of thirst. Several of the wagons had to be abandoned including the Reeds' cherished "pioneer palace."

As the last week of September approached, it became clear that the remaining supplies would be insufficient to complete the journey. Riders Charles Stanton and William McCutcheon were sent ahead to California to bring back assistance. Meanwhile the exhausted Donner Party pushed on, finally rejoining the main wagon trail near the Humboldt River on September 26. Hastings's "shortcut" had proven more than one hundred miles longer than the old trail, and it had cost them several weeks they could ill afford to lose. Already some of the distant peaks were tinged with snow. Time was running out.

As they lunged for the Sierras, desperately hoping to get there ahead of the first heavy snows, tempers began to fray. A fight broke out when James Reed attempted to restrain a teamster named John Snyder, who was beating exhausted oxen with the butt of his whip. When the fight was over, Snyder lay dead with Reed's hunting knife buried in his chest. Reed was accused of murder, and some wanted to hang him. Instead, he was banished and forced to ride off into the wilds to a fate most thought little better than hanging. Ironically, this tragedy would end up saving the lives of half the members of the otherwise doomed Donner Party.

Misfortune continued to dog the little wagon train. A week after Snyder's death, a Paiute Indian raiding party killed nearly two dozen oxen with poisoned arrows. Even so, the company managed to stagger on to the Truckee River and the foot of the Sierra which they reached on October 16. Then, just three days later, their luck seemed to change when Charles Stanton returned from Sutter's Fort on the far side of the mountains with seven mules loaded with food and supplies. Spirits soared. Perhaps they would reach safety after all.

After several days of rest, the Donner Party made its final push on the Sierra passes, with Stanton and a pair of Indian guides in the lead. It seemed for a while as if they would surely make it over, but then it began to snow. Starting out as just a few scattered flakes, the storm quickly grew in intensity, and soon the very air had turned white. Just a few hundred feet from the summit of what is today called Donner Pass, axle-deep drifts brought the wagons to a dead stop. There was no choice now but to turn the wagons around and head back down the mountain. The race was over. The snow had won.

Pitching a rough camp beside Truckee Lake deep in the lofty Sierra, the Donner Party tried to settle in for the winter. What shelter they managed to build for themselves offered little protection from the gathering cold or the nearly constant sleet and snow. There were no medical supplies, and what little food remained soon ran out. By December, most were living off boiled leather, leaves, bark, and bones. Halfway through the month, people began to die. The first was Balis Williams, one of Reed's hired hands.

Few believed that the party could survive the entire winter, and about a week before Christmas, a group of ten men and five women tried to walk out over the mountain. They called themselves the "Forlorn Hope" after a military expression often used to describe the first troops chosen to scale the walls of an enemy fort. Much like grimly determined soldiers facing the bullets and bayonets of a well-fortified enemy, the members of the Donner Forlorn Hope fully expected to die. Even so, they figured anything was better than languishing beside the cold, rock-hard lake waiting to starve to death or freeze.

Using makeshift snowshoes, and with Stanton in the lead, the Forlorn Hope trudged over the mountains for more than a week. Eventually, Stanton was blinded by the snow. Too sick and exhausted to continue, he begged the others to leave him to his fate and push ahead. Reluctantly, they did.

Nine days out, the remaining members of the Forlorn Hope finally gave up and stopped walking. Most had not eaten for days, and all understood only too well that they were dying. On Christmas Eve, with snow and sleet pelting down and no hope whether forlorn or otherwise remaining, someone made a suggestion. They would draw straws to see who would be killed, cooked, and eaten.

Some may have argued against the idea, but in the end, the plan was accepted. A man named Patrick Dolan drew the short straw, but none of the others could bring themselves to kill him. The next day, he died anyway along with three other members of the group. Although some accounts disagree, legend holds that all four were butchered and eaten.

With their strength thus renewed, the remnants of the Forlorn Hope pressed onward through the bleak mountains. Over the next few days, several more people are said to have been eaten, including a half-frozen Indian guide murdered for his flesh. Then on January 17, a month after they had left the Donner Party camp, the seven remaining members of the group found a settler's cabin in the western foothills of the Sierra. Strangely enough, five of the survivors were women. All but two of the men had died.

Stranded in the Sierra during the winter of 1846–1847, starving members of the fabled Donner Party battled drifts that reached the height of these stumps, perhaps fifteen feet or more. Some say that, when the food ran out, these desperate pioneers relied on their dead comrades for sustenance.

Back at Truckee Lake, things had gotten even worse, if such were possible, as more and more men, women, and children died. After a while, the living stopped trying to chop through the ice to bury their dead companions. The frozen bodies were simply left on the bare ground and covered with blankets or heaps of snow. Some of the bodies disappeared and may have been carried off by animals, but dark claims were later made concerning what had happened to them.

Spread out in two or more camps along or near the lake, most members of the party had largely stopped communicating with one another. They simply had no energy left for talk or for moving back and forth between the camps. They had also stopped looking up toward the blinding white summit to watch for a relief party. They had long since lost all hope of rescue.

Unbeknownst to anyone at Truckee Lake, however, an attempt had been made to reach them as far back as November. It had been led by none other than James Reed. Banished from the Donner wagon train for killing John Snyder, Reed had pressed on alone, reaching John Sutter's Fort on the far side of the Sierra in late October. The other pioneers who knew the Donner Party was still out on the trail had waited and watched, but no one had tried to put together a relief effort. Desperate to save his wife, Margaret, and their five children, Reed quickly organized one, but a few days out, Reed and his companions ran head on into a blizzard and were forced to turn back.

Even history now turned against the Donner Party. War had broken out between the United States and Mexico, and the fighting had spread to California. By the time Reed returned to Sutter's Fort to seek additional help in reaching his family and friends, every available able-bodied man in the area had gone off to fight the Mexicans. With the passes clogged by snow, Reed had no choice but to wait.

The waiting ended when the battered and bleeding remnants of the Forlorn Hope arrived on the west slope of Sierra and spread word of the Donner Party's plight. It soon became obvious to Reed and others that the remaining members of the Donner Party could not survive without immediate assistance. By early February, two separate relief columns—one of them led by Reed—were pushing eastward through the mountains. They did not reach Truckee Lake until late in the month, and what they found there horrified them. Many had died and some of those who still lived had begun to eat the dead.

To his immense relief, Reed found among the living his beloved wife and children. What food the rescue parties could spare was distributed among the gaunt survivors. Then, two dozen of them were evacuated over the mountains to safety.

For those left behind at the Lake, the horrors were not over. They could only hope that additional rescue parties were on the way. They were, but by the time they arrived in April, many more had died. In all, forty-one members of the original Donner party perished. Among the dead were George Donner; his wife, Tamsen; and four of their children.

Another forty-six members of the Donner party survived to reach California and make what they could of the dreams it still held for them. As he had planned all along, James Reed went into business and earned a second fortune from buying and selling land. Settling south of San Francisco Bay, he became a leading citizen of the town of San Jose.

Lansford Hastings, whose false shortcut led to so much suffering and death, never admitted having played any role in the tragedy. He practiced law in San Francisco for a time, but had very little success. Sympathetic to the Confederacy during the Civil War, he later suggested that defeated Southerners should consider moving to Brazil where slavery was still legal. He even wrote a book on the subject called the *Emigrant's Guide to Brazil.*

Not surprisingly, few of the Donner Party survivors would talk openly about their experiences. One of those who did was Lewis Keseburg, but his admission to having eaten human flesh earned him no friends and he soon fell silent on the subject. Keseburg struck it rich during the Gold Rush and later opened a successful restaurant in Sacramento. Keseburg's restaurant was famous for its steaks.

CHAPTER 8

The Rainman Who Flooded San Diego

The American West is mostly dry, and in many places it doesn't rain enough during the summer for farmers to produce a good crop. Droughts are common, and when they last long enough, they can ruin small agricultural communities and bankrupt entire regions. During the late nineteenth and early twentieth centuries, a series of long droughts hit the West hard. People prayed for rain, and when that didn't work, they sometimes hired rainmakers.

A peculiar brand of huckster who traded on the ignorance, gullibility, and desperation of simple people, rainmakers promised downpours in exchange for a substantial payment to be received only if it actually rained. Once he had a signed contract in hand, the rainmaker would regularly build bonfires and add special chemicals to the flames, blast away at the clouds with magic cannon, or perform some sort of hocus-pocus until it either rained or it didn't. If the drought proved stubborn, the rainmaker lost nothing more than a few dollars' worth of inexpensive minerals or gunpowder, and if it rained, he pocketed a handsome reward. Since it would always rain some of the time, either with or without the chemicals or cannon, these charlatans had a very profitable business going. Of course, they couldn't actually make it rain, but that never seemed to matter to farmers whose parched fields had received a good soaking.

According to legend, however, there was one rainmaker who was for real, who could and did make it rain hundreds of times in hundreds of places. It is said he was so good at coaxing the heavens to open their gates that his neighbors in San Diego once accused him of flooding them out of their homes. His name was Charles Hatfield. When Hatfield was born one dark and stormy night during the 1870s in Fort Scott way out on the Kansas plains, it was pouring rain—buckets of it. Supposedly, he came into the world at a crack of thunder, an appropriate entrance for a man who, for nearly all of his eighty-three years, would be closely associated with storms and cloudbursts.

Hatfield's father was Stephen Hatfield, a Singer sewing machine salesman from the Midwest, where most people relied on their crops for a living. If it didn't rain enough or the rains came at the wrong time, folks went hungry. Hatfield was still a boy in 1886 when his father brought him and his family to California, a place where rain and drought were even bigger concerns than in the Midwest.

Once in the Golden State, Stephen Hatfield bought an olive farm and then later tried his hand at growing apricots. He

In 1916 the citizens of San Diego hired rainmaker Charles Hatfield to fill parched municipal reservoirs and then reneged on the deal when the city was hit by severe flooding. The 1935 Bert Wheeler and Robert Woolsey comedy *The Rainmaker* may have been inspired by the Hatfield story. Notice that the movie is being used to sell people on the Morton Salt slogan "When it rains, it pours."

never relied entirely on farming, though, and dabbled in real estate on the side. He also continued to sell sewing machines for Singer. From his father, Charles Hatfield no doubt learned about the importance of water to farmers, to city dwellers—to everyone—and that being a good salesman counted for a lot no matter what one happened to be selling. The son of a farmer himself, the elder Hatfield also taught his son to look elsewhere for a career. There were many ways to make money and earn a living in California, and farming was the hardest of them all.

The young Hatfield apparently took this advice to heart for he was no farmer. Instead he was an avid reader, thinker, and tinkerer. The twentieth century was dawning, and exciting new scientific discoveries were being made nearly every day. Louis Pasteur had found a way to keep milk fresh, and Thomas Edison had invented a means of converting electricity to light. Why couldn't someone find a way to make it rain? Hatfield thought he might just be that someone.

Hatfield was fascinated by the experiments of meteorological theorists—some might consider them kooks and charlatans—who said they knew how to turn an ordinary white, fluffy cloud into a dark, angry rain cloud, how to turn a dry day into a rainy one, how to put an end to drought. He read the texts of Edward Powers on the infant science of meteorology and poured over the writings of Louis Gathmann who had noticed that clouds typically formed after large numbers of artillery shells exploded on a battlefield. He learned that Lucien Blake had tried to make rain by dusting clouds with "smoke balls" made of turpentine and sawdust and that Robert Dyrenforth, with the help of a $7,000 federal grant, had tried to wring moisture from clouds by detonating bombs made of potassium chlorate and petroleum in high-altitude balloons.

Hatfield had heard about a supposedly secret rainmaking formula developed by Frank Melbourne, who came to the United States from Australia, the world's driest continent. Dust-dry farming communities throughout the Midwest paid Melbourne to make it rain on their wilting crops. He prospered for a time, but then his formula—a smoldering mix of muriatic acid, hydrogen gas, and zinc—was published in the *Farmer's Almanac.* Melbourne's rainmaking business failed, which from the point of view of farmers was probably just as well. His formula smelled really bad but didn't produce much in the way of moisture.

Hatfield thought he could do better. On April 1—April Fool's Day—1902, he climbed to the top of a windmill tower on his father's property, laid out some metal pans filled with water, and added to them a number of chemicals which have never to this day been identified. Then he built a small fire beneath the pans. It was a moist day and there were only a few clouds in the sky, but Hatfield was confident that he could generate more. As the acrid smoke rose from the hot pans and drifted up into the sky, Hatfield replenished the chemicals to keep his formula at full strength. He was sure he was about to accomplish what so many others had tried but failed to achieve. He was about to make it rain.

And rain it did. First came fog, and then clouds began to form overhead and it started to drizzle. The drizzle turned into a shower, which did not last long, but it was enough to be measured by Hatfield's rain gauge. When the shower had passed, the gauge read three one-hundredths of an inch. Hatfield told this story many times. His success, he said, had come as a complete surprise. He had not really believed his formula would work, at least not the first time he tried it.

Perhaps wary of a mistake similar to the one that Frank Melbourne had made—and of seeing his formula published in the *Farmer's Almanac*—Hatfield never revealed it to anyone. He would only say that it consisted of twenty-seven separate chemicals. Mix them together in just the right quantities and you could bring rain, but not unless there was sufficient moisture present in the atmosphere. He did not make it rain, he said, so much as he made the rain come to him.

During the 1890s, Southern California endured seven long years of drought. The grass in pastures dried to stubble, cattle starved, and crops drowned in dust. It was the worst drought in over thirty years, and churches declared a special day of prayer hoping heaven would open up and release its precious rain. Perhaps the prayers were answered in the form of what Hatfield called his "moisture accelerator."

By this time Hatfield had followed his father into the sewing machine business and was working for Singer in Los Angeles, but he was also using his spare time to perfect his rainmaking technique. His study of meteorology had convinced him that he would get better results if he were higher up. After all, it rains more in the mountains than on the plains. So, he established a base at La Crescenta in the hills near Los Angeles, and there he built a tower in which to mix and heat his chemicals. No less tired of the drought than anyone else in Southern California, his boss at Singer had offered him $50 if he could make it rain within five days. Hatfield did it in two.

The rains came hard and steady, not only to Los Angeles, but to towns as far away as San Luis Obispo, about two hundred miles up the coast. The weather forecasters had predicted rain for the northern part of the state but not for the south. They were wrong. It poured, temporarily breaking the drought and bringing tears of relief to the eyes of farmers. Newspapers stories concerning Hatfield's valiant rainmaking efforts at La Crescenta soon made him a celebrity. People really believed that the sewing machine salesman had made it rain.

George Franklin, head of the California office of the National Weather Bureau, called Hatfield an "alchemist." He pointed out that the storm had originated in the northwest and could not possibly have been caused by a pan full of chemicals on a tower in the California hills. But who were people to believe? It had rained hadn't it? And the weather bureau had said it would not. Naturally, enough, Hatfield had no compunction about claiming credit, along with the $50 his boss had offered him. All he had needed, he said, was a little moisture in the air.

"I do not fight nature," said Hatfield. "I woo her by natural means."

Hatfield would attempt to seduce nature once again the following year. This time he would send his chemicals into the atmosphere in an attempt to win a $1,000 prize offered by the citizens of Los Angeles. To earn the prize—an enormous wind-fall at the time—Hatfield needed to produce eighteen inches of rain. He succeeded, and in doing so made his a household name.

Stores started selling Hatfield umbrellas and whenever a little rain fell, people would say it was "Hatfielding outside." Suddenly, "Professor" Charles Hatfield was a star!

Hatfield did have setbacks, however. One of these came during the 1890s Gold Rush in the Canadian Klondike. Placer and hydraulic gold-mining operations in the Klondike depended upon access to plentiful water, but a drought had brought gold production almost to a standstill. Hired to produce rain for $10,000, Hatfield arrived, set up his towers, mixed his chemicals, and waited. Nothing happened. After a few weeks, Hatfield left the Klondike high and dry and headed for home.

Having returned to the more familiar environment of California, Hatfield then resumed the work he knew best: making rain for farmers, According to the many stories concerning him, he brought rain to farming communities in the San Joaquin, in the Los Angeles Valley, and throughout the West from Oregon to Texas. Hatfield understood farmers, and he knew there was one commodity they needed at least as much as water: hope. So he sold them hope, and in the eyes of those who happened to believe, perhaps a little rain on the side. Hatfield continued in this way for years making rain when and where he could and perhaps selling the occasional sewing machine. Then, in 1915 he was asked to come to the rescue of one of California's largest cities—San Diego.

San Diego sits by the Pacific Ocean, and it was once a lush oasis of willows and Torrey pines where wild grapevines grew along the edges of beaches and cliffs. However, the weather seems to have gotten drier since Spanish colonial times, and the growing city was spreading out over a series of arid mesas and canyons. Water was scarce. Usually, it rained during the winter, but the runoff was not enough to serve the city's needs, and by the middle of the summer, lakes and streams were bone dry. The nearest major river was the Colorado, more than 150 miles away, and attempts to tap that resource invariably failed. One such effort during the early 1900s led to a disastrous flood which drowned a quarter of a million acres of prime Imperial Valley farmland (read more about this calamity in *Disasters and Heroic Rescues of California* by Ray Jones and Joe Lubow). But something had to be done because San Diego was growing fast, and the need for water was growing with it.

Tourism was on the rise in San Diego, and in 1915, the city decided to promote itself by launching a heavily publicized International Exposition. Everyone in America and, indeed, the world was invited to the big show. What was not widely known outside Southern California, however, was that the entire region was in the midst of a major drought. The area around San Diego had been especially hard hit. Would there be enough water to slack the thirst of all those thousands of visitors or to support the tremendous growth the exposition was expected to bring?

To make sure there would be plenty of water, the city council had purchased the largest private water company in the area—Southern California Mountain Water—which had built dams and reservoirs in the hills east of San Diego. The water flowed down to the city through a vast system of flumes and conduits. There should be no problem, the council concluded, so long as the reservoirs remained full. Soon, however, they were very much alarmed to discover that the water level in the important Morena Reservoir in the Laguna Mountains was dangerously low. If water usage continued at the current high rates, this reservoir and others would soon be empty. There would be no water for the fountains on the exposition grounds, and visitors might have nothing to drink but sarsaparilla. In desperation, city officials turned to a rainmaker, the most famous one in the world—Charles Hatfield.

Engineers figured it would take about fifty inches of rain in the mountains to fill the 15-billion-gallon reservoir. Hatfield was given a full year to make his method work. If the necessary rain fell and the reservoir was full by December 20, 1916, Hatfield would receive $10,000. If he couldn't fill it, the rainmaker would receive nothing. The deal sounded very good to the San Diego council. If things worked out as planned, the city would pay only about one penny for each fifteen thousand gallons of water it received. On the other hand, if Hatfield couldn't produce, then the city would pay nothing. What was there to lose?

Seeing the possibility of a $10,000 payday, Hatfield quickly got down to work. At the Morena Reservoir he built two towers, one for his chemicals and another one to hide his activities from a curious public. Atop a twelve-foot square platform, Hatfield laid out his cast-iron pans, added his chemicals—in this case he had decided they should be double strength—applied heat, and waited. Filled with acrid smoke, the air around the platform smelled terrible, but no rain fell. Christmas came and went, and still no rain. Then on December 31, the last day of 1915, there were showers. These did a little to relieve the drought, but not much. People had begun to wonder if Hatfield was just another charlatan after all. Their doubts would soon be permanently erased.

About the middle of January, it started to rain again, and this time, Southern California was in for something more than just light showers. Torrents fell and reservoir levels surged. Convinced that he could coax the clouds to release even more of their bounty, Hatfield kept filling his pans with chemicals. He told reporters that they "hadn't seen anything yet."

Apparently, Hatfield was right. It had been a very long time since anyone in Southern California had seen so much water fall out of the sky. The deluge turned the streets of San Diego to rivers and the deserts to the east and south to oceans of mud. The runoff rushed down the mountain slopes to fill normally dry arroyos and gullies. The San Diego River surged over it banks and began to flood adjacent residential areas. Bridges were threatened, and some were lost. Downtown San Diego was littered with abandoned cars and debris left behind by the rushing water. For a while, people were forced to use boats to get from place to place.

Although many telephone lines were down, Hatfield somehow managed to get through to a *San Diego Union* reporter. "I just wanted to tell you that it is only sprinkling now," he told the reporter.

"Are you kidding?" asked the reporter.

"Never more serious in my life," said Hatfield. "Just hold your horses until I show you a real rain."

The rain slackened for several days, but then started up again in earnest about a week later. No one wanted to see more rain just yet, but it poured down anyway, completing the earlier catastrophe. In the country, farmers were flooded out of their homes, their crops ruined and their livestock drowned, and in the city people watched in alarm as the river once more rose out of its banks. So much water gushed into the reservoirs that city employees scrambled to open flood gates and relieve the strain on hard-pressed dams. The resulting floodwaters swept away bridges and forced San Diego officials to evacuate large portions of the city. Up at the Morena Reservoir, however, Charles Hatfield was smiling in satisfaction. The reservoir had been filled to the brim. He had met the terms of his contract and earned his reward nearly eleven months ahead of schedule.

Hatfield dumped his chemicals, buried his pans, cleaned himself up, and headed for San Diego, where he had expected to be treated like a hero. Instead he was regarded as a maniac, a villain who had destroyed half the city. People were in a very ugly mood, and fearing that an angry mob would form and possibly lynch him, Hatfield slipped out of town in disguise.

Perhaps not surprisingly, city officials refused to pay Hatfield for his services. They did so, not on the grounds that he had nearly drowned them, but rather because he was unable to prove that he had either made it rain or increased the volume of the rain. For Hatfield, that was perhaps just as well. If on the one hand he could not force the city to keep its part of the bargain, then neither could San Diego's rain-beleaguered residents sue him for bringing a calamity down on their heads. The storms and floods of January and February 1916 were put down by one and all to an accident of nature or, as some called it, an "act of God."

So whose act was it? Nature's? God's? Or Hatfield's? Probably we will never know for certain. Hatfield died in 1958, never having revealed his secret formula to anyone but his brother Paul, who had occasionally helped him with his rainmaking. The secret of the formula died along with Paul Hatfield in 1974, but not the legend of the rainmaker who flooded San Diego.

CHAPTER 9

Gunfight at Mussel Slough

A historical marker stands along a road just outside the town of Hanford in California's San Joaquin Valley. Placed here to mark what it refers to as the "Mussel Slough Tragedy," the marker reads as follows: "Here on May 11, 1880, during a dispute over land titles between settlers and railroads, a fight broke out during which seven men lost their lives—two deputy U.S. marshals and five ranchers. The legal struggle over titles was finally settled by a compromise."

These few words can hardly convey what took place here on that day more than 130 years ago, but it is possible to imagine the scene—the chaos, the gun smoke, the smell of exploded gunpowder, the cries of frightened horses, the screams of wounded men, and the blood draining away into the dust. It was like the fabled gunfight at the O.K. Corral only more violent, if such were possible. Four men died at the O.K. Corral on October 26, 1881, but seven had died at the Mussel Slough confrontation the previous year. Both gunfights are legendary, but the one at Mussel Slough may have been more meaningful.

When Wyatt Earp, Doc Holliday, and Earp's two brothers took on the Clantons and the McLaurys at Tombstone, Arizona, there were no grand principles involved. Four part-time lawmen had a shootout with a gang of armed thugs, and that was about the extent of it. The gunfight at Mussel Slough, on the other hand, pitted a band of farmers against a group of lawmen who had been sent there by the railroads to foreclose on their land. As the farmers saw it, the railroads were trying to steal their land, and they were willing to pull their rifles and six shooters off the wall and die, if necessary, to defend their homes and fields. It was, in short, a confrontation between poor homesteaders and the steely forces of corporate greed, or at least, that is the myth.

The story of the Mussel Slough gunfight has been told and retold in the press and by several generations of novelists and historians. No fewer than five novels have celebrated the event: *Blood Money* by V. C. Morrow, *Driven from the Sea to Sea* by C. C. Post, *Feud of Oakfield Creek* by Josiah Royce, *First the Blade* by May Merrill Miller, and *The Octopus* by Frank Norris, which was written more than twenty years after the smoke cleared at Mussel Slough. These fictional accounts tended to endorse the notion that the gunfight was a collision between good, represented by the farmers, and evil, represented by the railroads. Readers were more ready to accept that vision of the incident, and no less a bookworm than President Theodore

Roosevelt would be deeply moved by *The Octopus,* which like most books, he inhaled almost in a single sitting. The story of the gunfight as depicted by Norris would deeply influence Roosevelt, causing him to be even more inclined to seek legislation likely to rein in overly powerful tycoons and corporations.

But what actually happened at Mussel Slough? Who fired the first shots, and why? And who, if anyone, got the better of the clash?

The story of the gunfight at Mussel Slough began long before the farmers and lawmen grabbed their guns and started pulling triggers. It could be said to have been set in motion when the first Europeans set foot in America intent on claiming free land and making it their own. However, the chain of events that led to gunfire in the San Joaquin can be traced more directly to 1862, when Congress enacted two immensely important pieces of legislation, both of them aimed at building up the country. One of these was the Homestead Act, which offered more or less free land to poor farm families willing to live on the property, improve it, and make it fruitful. The other was the Railroad Act, which parceled out large tracts of land to railroads to help them pay for laying tract into mostly unsettled country. At first glance, these two groundbreaking laws would appear complementary—the Homestead Act provided land for farmers while the Railroad Act encouraged the development of a transportation system to help them get their crops to market. Instead, these two well-meaning laws laid the groundwork for conflict. That is because, all too often, the land given to the rail-road companies was already occupied by homesteaders.

Homesteading was a hard and often unsuccessful under-taking. In the Central Valley of California, for instance, long, rainless summers and the lack of a dependable water supply for livestock and irrigation made producing a profitable crop a hit or miss affair. Also troubling was the hostility of local ranchers who looked upon the newcomers as interlopers likely to fence the land and bring an end to the cowboy way of life.

"The stockmen looked upon us as intruders, and discour-aged us all they could," said Mary Chambers, who with her husband, Frank, attempted to homestead land in the San Joa-quin. The ranchers told the Chamberses their land was useless for farming and that the couple would certainly starve to death.

"We did not believe," said Chambers. "We with our energy and perseverance would make the wilderness blossom and bear. Alas, how we flattered ourselves!"

Sure enough, the Chamberses could barely eke out a living, but they survived, and as more and more homesteaders drifted into the area, a cooperative spirit emerged. These pioneering farmers helped one another through the hard times and pitched in to dig a canal and bring irrigation water from the King River. They also sought legal protection from the ranchers who habitu-ally allowed their free-ranging cattle to trample crops. Under the provisions of the recently enacted California Fence Law, cattlemen were forced to corral their herds or pay damages to the farmers. Before long the San Joaquin began to bloom. Wheat was especially abundant, and the Mussel Slough area in particular began to be called the "Breadbasket of California."

The farmers of the San Joaquin and Mussel Slough may not have known it at the time, but a herd of steel horses was headed in their direction. Encouraged and enriched by the federal Pacific Railroad Act of 1862, four Sacramento businessmen were laying tracks throughout California and the West. Their names were Leland Stanford, Mark Hopkins, Hollis P. Huntington, and Charles Crocker, and they not only built railroads but also grabbed up large blocks of land wherever and whenever they could.

Having served briefly as California's governor during the 1860s, Leland Stanford was president of the Union Pacific Railroad. Mark Hopkins, known for his ability to squeeze every last penny out of a dollar, was the company's treasurer. Through a separate company Charles Crocker headed the actual construction of tunnels, bridges, tracks, and roadbeds. Hollis Huntington fronted for the others in the all-important arenas of the U.S. Congress and the California legislature. These four rich and powerful men formed a sort of club that they enjoyed referring to as "The Associates." The press and the public, on the other hand, simply called them "The Big Four."

The Big Four were so big that they were entrusted by Congress with construction of the western portion of the Transcontinental Railroad. By the time the line was completed and the Golden Spike was driven in 1876, the four were very rich, but they saw no reason why they shouldn't continue to cash in on their accomplishments. To do this they began to extend their tracks like tentacles into every farming community in the West. People began to refer to this rapidly spreading railroad behemoth as the "Octopus." Among the fertile valleys that came within the grasp of the Octopus were the San Joaquin and Mussel Slough.

The Big Four had received an enormous San Joaquin land grant to help finance construction of its tracks there. As a result, some homesteaders found themselves squatting on land that no longer belonged to the federal government but, rather, was owned by the railroad. Since the rail lines needed farmers to turn a profit on the movement of crops, goods, and people, the company agreed to sell the land back to the homesteaders for as little as $2.50 an acre. To preserve their farms and their way of life, most agreed to pay. In fact, many of the homesteaders had been lured to the area in the first place by a railroad pamphlet offering to sell the land for just such a price.

However, something very strange—and seemingly very unfair—happened before the transactions became official. The homesteaders had greatly improved the land by building houses, barns, and fences and by successfully tilling the soil. Together with the impending arrival of the railroad itself, these improvements caused the recognized value of these properties to soar to $20, $30, or even $40 an acre. Few, if any, farmers could pay such a price, and when they began to receive enormous bills from the railroads, the homesteaders were appalled. Understandably, they felt cheated.

The Chambers family got stuck with a price they could not possibly meet: $22 an acre.

"And why?" asked Mary Chambers, although she understood only too well. "Because we had a house, a barn, orchard, alfalfa pasture, flower garden, ditches, and a well-cultivated farm. Now, just as we were getting our heads above water, here comes the demand: $22 per acre or leave the land."

The railroad officials were adamant. Pay our price or get out, they said, and they meant it. The homesteaders protested, and when the railroad refused to back down, they grew increasingly enraged. A group of six hundred of them banded together under the banner of a civic organization they called the Settler's League. To defend their rights, they went to court arguing that the railroad had promised them the land prices would remain low. Improvements made by the farmers themselves were not supposed to have been considered when setting the price.

Although the homesteaders were hopeful, they were going up against an intractable and immensely powerful foe. Stanford and company had friends in the highest political offices, they could afford the best lawyers in California if not the entire country, and if necessary, they had money for bribes. The farmers never had a chance. One judge and court after another decided in favor of the railroad, and in the end, Stanford and the Union Pacific ended up with legal title to the land. Even so, most of the homesteaders refused to either pay up or leave. A showdown was inevitable.

Not all of the farmers in the Mussel Slough area were members of the Settler's League. At least nineteen local families had sided with the railroads, and for obvious reasons they were not well liked by their neighbors. Some were threatened, and vigilante groups ranged across the land vowing to take measures against anyone who refused to support the league.

By the late spring of 1880, the legal remedies sought by the homesteaders had run their course. The farmers knew that the time for action on both sides was rapidly approaching. Even so, as the sun arced past noon on the fateful day of May 11, 1880, the members of the Settler's League were not up in arms. Instead, they were attending a picnic.

United States Marshal Alonzo Poole knew about the picnic, and for that very reason he chose this particular afternoon to ride into Mussel Slough with eviction notices in hand. Accompanying Poole were William H. Clark, a land appraiser, as well as Mills Hartt and Walter Crow, who had purchased from the railroad two key properties occupied by members of the Settler's League. The homesteaders who were to be evicted were Henry Brewer and J. O. Storer. Under orders from Federal Court Judge Lorenzo Sawyer, a Stanford political appointee, Poole was prepared to enforce the evictions at the point of a gun if necessary.

When news of Poole's arrival reached the ears of league members, the picnic chicken, cakes, and pies were pushed aside.

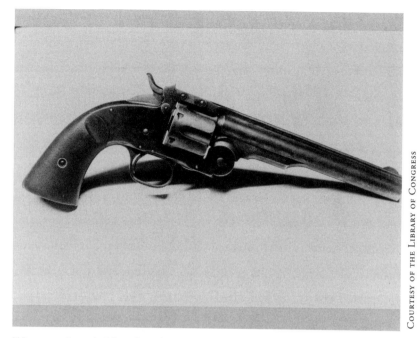

When an attempted farm foreclosure erupted into violence at Mussel Slough in 1880, some of the gunmen likely relied on six-shooters like this one, wielded elsewhere but at about that same time by famed outlaw Jesse James.

A sizable group of farmers then armed themselves and hurried off to defend their neighbor's property. They found Poole at Henry Brewer's farm, where they confronted the marshal and his companions. Poole was personally sympathetic to the settlers and tried his best to calm the crowd. In the steadiest voice he could muster, he ordered them to disarm and disperse. They refused. The settlers then demanded that Poole give up his weapon, but he in turn, refused. Meanwhile Crow and Hartt had gotten into a heated argument with the settlers over who owned what and tensions threatened to boil over.

At that point, there happened an accident of the sort that can put a match to dry kindling and turn a heated though blood-less confrontation into a massacre. A skittish horse was spooked by something—nobody ever knew exactly what—and knocked Marshal Poole to the ground. In an instant, gunmen on both sides had drawn their pistols or leveled rifles and begun to fire. Witnesses would later disagree on who had fired the first shot, but some said that Hartt and settler James Harris, who had long hated one another, drew their guns and fired simultaneously. Regardless of who fired first, several dozen more shots followed. Gun smoke obscured the scene as bullets zinged through the air, ricocheted off rocks, and tore into human flesh. The screams of wounded and dying men could be heard even above the staccato bark of the gunfire. Then, less than a minute after the fight had begun, it was all over.

On the ground lay the bodies of five farmers: Harris, Archibald McGregor, Daniel Kelly, Ivar Knutson, and John Henderson. Also dead was Mills Hartt, who would never take possession of the property he had so recently purchased from the railroad. Neither would Walter Crow, an expert marksman who was said to have done most of the killing. Having emerged unwounded from the initial shootout, Crow fled through a nearby wheat field, but the settlers were gunning for him. He was later found some distance away with a bullet in his back.

After a thorough investigation, the law came down solidly on the side of the railroad. Stanford and the Big Four made sure of that. Although no one was convicted of murder, five of the settlers, including John J. Doyle, James N. Patterson, John D. Powell, Wayman L. Pryor, and William Braden were convicted of obstructing a federal marshal. They served eight months in the Santa Clara jail and were afterward welcomed as heroes when they returned to Mussel Slough.

Faced with an avalanche of negative publicity, the railroads reduced the prices they had asked the settlers to pay for their land, but never gave the slightest ground on the question of who actually had owned it in the first place. Many of the settlers stayed on and paid off the debt on their land. Others, who could not pay, drifted away.

Stanford, Crocker, Hopkins, and Huntington were, of course, never charged with anything but were nonetheless convicted in the court of public opinion. Anti-railroad sentiment grew, not just in California, but all across the country. And after 1901 when a progressive Republican president took office in the person of Theodore Roosevelt, new laws began to be enacted to limit the power of monopolistic corporations and the barons of commerce. Legend, it seems, can accomplish more than bullets.

Six victims of the gunfight at Mussell Slough were initially laid out in the shade of a huge oak tree that grew beside Henry Brewer's house. It later came to be called the Tragedy Oak, and it stood right up until the 1990s, when it was finally blown over in a storm. The old Brewer farm is gone as well.

CHAPTER 10

California's Very Own Pearl Harbor

E arly on the morning of February 25, 1942, air-raid sirens blared all over the Los Angeles metropolitan area. People throughout the city tumbled out of bed, threw open their shutters, and peered up at the sky to see if they could tell what on earth was happening. Was Los Angeles under attack? Were the Japanese in the process of bombing the City of Angels just like they had bombed Pearl Harbor less than three months earlier?

The people of California, indeed of the entire West Coast, had plenty of reason to be nervous. Military bases in California, Oregon, and Washington had been placed on a war footing in late November 1941, when the Japanese had broken off negotiations with the U.S. State Department. Then on December 7, Americans were stunned by the news that Japanese torpedo planes and bombers had severely damaged the U.S. Pacific Fleet stationed in Honolulu. This crippling blow, which of course led to an immediate declaration of war, appeared to have left Hawaii and the western U.S. wide open to further attacks.

Most considered it hardly worth asking *if* an attack would come. The important questions were *where* and *when.* Surely, if the Japanese could assemble a force powerful enough to hit the American fleet in Hawaii so hard, then they would soon strike the U.S. mainland as well. Los Angeles seemed a likely enough target.

Wild rumors flew. For instance, on December 8, the very day after the bombing of Pearl Harbor, there were rumors afoot that an attack on California was imminent. A Japanese aircraft carrier was said to have been spotted off the coast near San Francisco. Oakland closed its schools and, later, during the dinner hour, radio broadcasts stopped, sirens blared, and a blackout was enforced for more than three hours. The sirens, incidentally, were supplied by police cars, since a standard air-raid warning system was not yet in place.

The truth was, of course, that there was no Japanese aircraft carrier off the coast of California. Although civilians, and likely the U.S. military as well, had no way of knowing for sure, the nearest Imperial Navy carrier was more than three thousand miles west of San Francisco. Even so, U.S. Army technicians claimed to have tracked unidentified airplanes aloft as much as one hundred miles out in the Pacific.

Some in San Francisco eventually concluded that the whole thing had been a hoax. The Army angrily denied this. "You think it was a hoax?" fumed Lt. General John L. DeWitt. "It is damned nonsense for sensible people to assume that the Army and Navy would practice such a hoax on San Francisco."

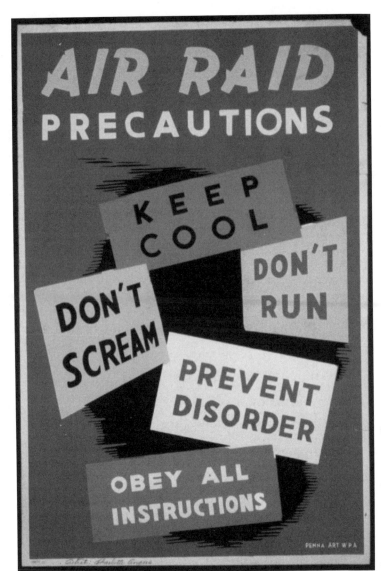

During World War II, Americans had cause to fear a Japanese air raid on the West Coast. Despite posters like this one, intended to promote a calm and orderly response, Los Angeles was thrown into a wild panic when antiaircraft guns went into action on the night of February 24–25, 1942. Apparently, the guns were firing at a stray weather balloon.

Regardless of whether there had or had not been Japanese planes on the way, invasion fever had California in its grip. December 9 brought word that as many as thirty-four enemy ships were poised just off the coast. Where were they and where did they intend to strike? No one could say for sure. If the enemy ships had ever been out there, they soon faded into the coastal fog.

The rumor mill kept on grinding. Some claimed there were secret Japanese airbases in California and, perhaps more ominously, that Japanese fishermen in California were secretly meeting with enemy ships offshore and providing them with food, fuel, and information to help them prepare for an attack. Some even believed the fishermen were mining harbors! While none of these rumors had any basis in fact, they increased the distrust that many Americans felt toward fellow citizens of Japanese descent, even those whose ancestors had come to the U.S. decades or even generations earlier.

During those heady weeks following December 7, no one was likely to forget that the nation was at war. If anyone needed a reminder, however, they got one shortly before Christmas when the oil tanker *Montebello* went down along the central California coast, the victim of a Japanese submarine attack. On December 24, another ship, the lumber freighter *Abaoroska* took a torpedo amidships, but miraculously did not sink. The latter attack, which killed a crewman, took place in the Catalina Channel, just west of Los Angeles.

Nearly two months would pass before the next significant enemy blow fell on California. It would hit an oil refinery just to the west of the scenic town of Santa Barbara and about sixty miles northwest of Los Angeles. At approximately 7 p.m. on February 23, 1942, just as President Franklin Roosevelt was about to deliver one of his famous fireside chats on radio, Mrs. George Heaney spotted what she believed was a submarine in the waters just off Ellwood Beach. Bob Miller, who was working at the Ellwood refinery that evening, also reported sighting the submarine. They could not be sure at first it was an enemy vessel, but any doubts about that evaporated as soon as shells started crashing down on the refinery. In all, sixteen shells were fired. Three of these shells struck the refinery destroying a pumping station about one thousand yards inland, but the remainder missed their marks. One fell on a ranch about three miles from the coast where it dug a hole nearly five feet deep but failed to explode. Having unleashed its attack, the submarine vanished into the vast Pacific.

According to historical accounts, the vessel in question was a Japanese I-17 Sensuikan-class submarine under the command of Kozo Nishino. In a bizarre coincidence, Commander Nishino had been captain of a Japanese oil tanker which had visited the Ellwood refinery during the 1930s. It had not been a pleasant visit for Nishino, who had slipped during the welcoming ceremony and fallen into a prickly-pear cactus. Workers on a nearby oil rig broke into guffaws at the sight of the proud commander having cactus spines plucked from his posterior. The shamefaced Nishino swore he would someday get even, and apparently he succeeded.

The early morning air-raid alert in Los Angeles came only two days after the attack on the Ellwood refinery. Like everyone in America, Angelinos were tense—after all, the nation was at war—but probably it would be too much to say they were frightened. Most had plenty of personal matters on their minds. Some had gotten jobs with suddenly prosperous local defense manufacturers such as Douglas Aircraft. Others were about to be in uniform and were busy putting their affairs in order and saying goodbye to family and friends. There was little time to waste on rumors, and earlier alerts had been based on little but rumor. However, the insistent sirens made this particular alert seem very much like the real thing. After they started up at around 2:20 a.m. on February 25, it is unlikely that anyone in Los Angeles got much sleep.

The military certainly believed something dangerous was in the air. On the previous evening naval intelligence officers had told the West Coast Defense Command that a Japanese attack might come at any time within the next ten hours. Midnight came and went and nothing happened, but at 2:15 a.m., radar detected an unidentified flying object out over the Pacific roughly 120 miles from Los Angeles. A citywide blackout was ordered and antiaircraft units were placed on Green Alert, which meant that they must be ready to fire on a moment's notice. Meanwhile, the Army's fighter planes were kept on the ground since there were simply too few of the precious interceptors to order them aloft without a sure target.

As the unidentified object approached the city, military commanders in the Los Angeles area were unsure of what to do. Then a mysterious thing happened—the object disappeared from radar screens. Even so, plenty of Angelinos had apparently seen it. The Information Center switchboard was flooded with calls from people who claimed they had seen something unusual in the skies above the city. Some said they had spotted airplanes over Long Beach and Los Angeles. Others had seen what appeared to be a balloon over Santa Monica.

As it turned out, the balloon—if that is what it was—was about to touch off a small war of its own. No one is certain who gave the order to fire, but four separate antiaircraft batteries suddenly opened up on it, and after that, both the military and the city were plunged into chaos. On the following day, the *Los Angeles Times* put out a "War Extra" describing the scene as follows:

Roaring out of a brilliant moonlit sky, foreign aircraft flying in both large formations and singly flew over Southern California early today and drew heavy barrages of anti-aircraft fire—the first ever to sound over United States continental soil against an enemy invader . . . .

The spectacular anti-aircraft barrage came after the 14th Interceptor Command ordered the blackout when strange craft were reported over the coastline. Powerful searchlights from countless stations stabbed the sky with brilliant probing fingers while anti-aircraft batteries dotted the heavens with beautiful, if sinister, orange bursts of shrapnel.

In the streets of the city, police officers and civil defense workers struggled to enforce a total blackout. Cars turned off their lights and attempted to make headway in the dark, while at home, people put blankets over their windows. Meanwhile, searchlights swept back and forth across the sky searching for the illusive enemy. Nothing was spotted, but many believed there were hundreds of airplanes above the city flying at high altitude or just over the treetops.

"You knew it had to be serious," said John Hall, who was thirteen years old at the time and a junior air-raid warden. "I wanted to get dressed and join our block warden to help make sure all the lights were out and the blackout was working, but my mother wouldn't let me leave the house."

Young Hall nonetheless witnessed an exciting drama. "The sky was ablaze with both the searchlights and explosions," he said.

For three hours, antiaircraft gunners targeted the smoke of their own bursting shells that were caught in the searchlights, or they just fired out toward where the gunners and their control-lers thought they had seen something—anything. Then the first light of dawn began to drive away the phantoms and the gunfire tapered off. People looked up and saw nothing but blue sky and seagulls. Los Angeles had gone back to being—Los Angeles.

So said the *Los Angeles Times:*

No bombs were dropped and no airplanes shot down and, miraculously in terms of the tons of missiles hurled aloft, only two persons were reported wounded by falling shell fragments. Countless thousands of Southland residents, many of whom were late to work because of the traffic tie-up during the blackout, rubbed their eyes sleepily yesterday and agreed that regardless of the question of how "real" the air raid alarm may have been, it was "a great show" and "well worth losing a few hours' sleep."

Military officials, who are usually very good with numbers, eventually concluded that 1,440 rounds had been fired at the sky during the night. Nothing had been shot down other than, perhaps, a few high-flying birds. The only casualties were a pedestrian who had been hit in the head with shrapnel and a pair of motorists who had panicked and gotten themselves killed in traffic accidents.

Everywhere in Los Angeles on the bright winter morning of February 25, people tried to pry apart their drooping eyelids and keep themselves awake with pots of coffee. No one could find any bomb craters. What exactly had happened?

Government and military officials were asking the same thing. Who was responsible for this mess? Were there really enemy planes overhead? If so, then why didn't they show up on radar? Who gave the order to open fire and why? California congressmen demanded to know if the event had been "a practice raid, or a raid to throw a scare into 2,000,000 people, or a mistaken identity raid, or a raid to take away Southern California's war industries."

A U.S. Navy investigation eventually concluded that there had never been any enemy planes that night. It had all been just one big false alarm. However, there were still military officials—including some at the top—who clung to the notion that there had been enemy activity in the vicinity of Los Angeles, after all. Among those the Navy could not convince was Secretary of War Henry Stimson.

"Either they were commercial planes operated by an enemy from secret fields in California or Mexico, or they were light planes launched from Japanese submarines," Stimson argued. "In either case, the enemy's purpose must have been to locate antiaircraft defenses in the area or to deliver a blow at civilian morale."

The *Washington Post* responded to Stimson's statement, observing that his theory "explains everything except where the planes came from, whither they were going, and why no American planes were sent in pursuit of them." No one, including Stimson, could ever answer any of these questions. After the war was over, however, the Japanese may have cleared matters up a bit when they provided information indicating that there had been no attack on Los Angeles that night. There had been no Imperial Navy ships or planes anywhere near California.

One popular theory concerning the incident is stubborn, and it refuses to go away. A *Los Angeles Times* photograph taken on the morning of the "attack" shows something remarkable in the skies above the city. Often republished in magazines devoted to so-called UFO phenomena, it shows searchlights coming together over the city to form an enormous nine-legged spider. At the intersection of the lights is a mysterious disc-shaped object. The photo is slightly out of focus, so it is impossible to identify the object with any certainty. Some who have studied this picture argue that it shows an alien ship hovering over the hills—not an alien ship as in "Japanese airplane," but alien as in "spaceship from another planet." Readers must decide for themselves.

CHAPTER 11

The Shadow God of California

Very few in California or elsewhere today have heard of Chinigchinich, and most would have difficulty pronouncing the name. They likely would be surprised to learn that Chinigchinich is a god once devoutly worshipped by Native American people in California. He may be venerated by some even to this day.

Who was—or is—this Chinigchinich? Unlike the gods that most people worship, he was not a native of the stars and sky, nor was he born on some holy mountain. Apparently, Chinigchinich started out as a man. According to the Luiseño people of Southern California, he was born among them in a remote part of what is today Los Angeles County.

Chinigchinich spent his life on earth as a prophet, ministering to his people, teaching them the good and correct way of living. Nothing is known about how he died except that he did not actually die. Instead he was lifted directly into the sky and transformed into the "heaven of the stars."

Afterward, Chinigchinich was everywhere at once and was able to keep a close watch on his people. He protected them and also made sure they lived their lives according to his teachings. If they did not, he sent poisonous snakes and other wild beasts to hurry them back to the path of righteousness. To punish severe violations he might send calamities such as earthquakes, fires, floods, and droughts.

If Native American people revere Chinigchinich today or remember him at all, they do not speak freely about him. Maybe it is forbidden to do so, or perhaps Chinigchinich has vanished back into the mythical shadows from which he emerged hundreds, if not thousands, of years ago. So why do we know anything at all about Chinigchinich? How do we even know his name?

What we know about Chinigchinich and the religion of the Luiseño people today we owe in large part to a Franciscan priest named Father Gerónimo Boscana. Ironically, Father Boscana came to California in order to convert the Indians here to another far more widespread religion—Roman Catholic Christianity. In 1806 Boscana arrived in Southern California where his order assigned him to the Mission San Juan Capistrano in what is today Orange County.

Capistrano was one of a string of missions the Spanish established along or near the California coast from San Diego in the south to Sonoma, a few dozen miles north of San Francisco. The missions were intended to help the Spanish solidify

During the early nineteenth century, a monk at the Capistrano Mission learned that local Indians believed in an ancient Southern California prophet whose teachings were not altogether dissimilar from those of Jesus, Mohammed, and Buddha. Shown here in ruins, the mission has been partially restored.

their hold on what was then a very remote province and also to spread Christianity to the Indians. Father Boscana probably considered his most important task to be that of a missionary. His purpose in coming to California was to spread the gospel of Christianity among what he then likely believed to be a simple, ignorant, and gullible people. When they came to the mission church, he may very well have smiled with satisfaction imagining them to be quite thoroughly and sincerely converted. At other times he may have taken genuine delight in the tribal dances and rituals he occasionally witnessed, believing these to be harmless celebrations of local culture which in no way conflicted with Christianity. It might never have entered his mind that he was witnessing the practice of an ancient and, to the Indians at least, very meaningful religion.

Father Boscana's view of these things would eventually undergo a radical transformation. The change began one day in 1812 when a letter arrived from Spain. It bore a request from the Spanish government for more information on its subjects in California. In essence, it was a questionnaire, perhaps not very unlike those that Americans receive from the Census Bureau every ten years. The responsibility for filling out the questionnaire fell upon Boscana, a man who took all of his duties quite seriously.

As part of this undertaking, Boscana began to question members of the Luiseño tribe who lived in and around the Capistrano Mission. He especially wanted to learn more about the dances and other rituals he had seen these people perform. He had been deeply impressed by the enthusiasm of the participants and the strong emotions they expressed. What did all this mean? Much to his surprise, ordinary Luiseños could not explain these things. He was told that these were mysteries fully understood only by Luiseño chiefs and shamans. No one could reveal their meaning, not even the shamans, without risking severe punishment and most likely death imposed by fierce animals sent by Chinigchinich.

There it was. The mention of the name Chinigchinich aroused a powerful curiosity in Boscana. Who or what was

Chinigchinich? The Indians pronounced the name with reverence, and in time, Boscana would come to regard it with a certain reverence himself. Eventually, Boscana was able to pry more and more information out of certain Indians who, in accepting Christianity, had begun to lose their fear of Chinigchinich's beasts. After devoting years of study to the subject of Luiseño beliefs, Boscana wrote a book entitled *Chinigchinich: a Historical Account of the Origin, Customs, and Traditions of the Indians at the Missionary Establishment of St. Juan Capistrano.* In it he does not clearly answer the question of Chinigchinich's identity, but rather, leaves that task to the reader.

Boscana's book included a pair of creation stories often told by Luiseño shamans. Much like the story of Adam and Eve in the *Book of Genesis,* they explain how the world and its people came into existence. The first of these stories goes somewhat as follows.

In the beginning there was a void, and in the void there were Brother Sky and Sister Earth, one above and one below. The void was dark, so Brother Sky created the sun. Sky and Earth then formed an incestuous union, and Sky gave birth to sand, soil, rocks, trees, shrubs, and grass. Later pregnancies brought animals into the world along with a man-like creature known as Oüiot.

Oüiot himself gave life to a race of beings "distinct from any which now inhabit the earth." Like Oüiot himself, these beings were part real and part imaginary. Oüiot set himself up as king of this new race, and a creature known as Coyote became his faithful assistant.

After much time had passed, the aging Oüiot was poisoned by his own children who wanted to seize the throne for themselves. Oüiot was cremated, and the anguished Coyote jumped into the flames rather than live without his beloved master. Following this drama a mysterious specter appeared. The frightened children of Oüiot asked the specter if he was the spirit of their murdered father perhaps come to seek revenge.

"No," the spirit replied, assuring them that he was a being of a much higher order than Oüiot. "My name is Chinigchinich. My habitation is above. I create all things."

Rather than punish the children of Oüiot, Chinigchinich changed them into spirit beings capable of causing the clouds to bring rain, the morning air to release dew, oak trees to produced acorns, ducks and geese to fly, and deer and rabbits to inhabit the fields and forests. Chinigchinich then created human beings out of clay taken from a nearby lake. He warned them to obey him and follow his teachings or he would send among them "bears to bite, serpents to sting, misfortunes, infirmities, and death." Certain members of Oüiot's family he turned into mortal humans who then became the tribal chiefs and shamans responsible for protecting their people and ensuring their obedience. Their secret knowledge of Chinigchinich and his teachings would be passed on from one generation to the next.

The second creation story retold in Father Boscana's book is somewhat like the first, but it has an extraordinary feature. The description it gave of Chinigchinich was less like that of an omnipotent god who came from the sky and more like that of a real man who may very well have once walked among the Indians and taught them a better way to live. Boscana wondered about this man. Who was he? Where did he come from? What message did he bring to his people? And where did he go?

In some respects, this second creation story begins much like the other. It is filled with descriptions of gods and spirit beings who create rocks, streams, and fishes and, eventually, men and women as well. As does the other story, it includes Oüiot who, in this case, is a cruel tyrant. Once again Oüiot is poisoned and cremated and, at the cremation ceremonies a godlike figure appears and assigns special tasks to those attending the funeral.

At this point, however, the second story diverges sharply from the first. Into it steps a prophet by the name of Chinigchinich—a man, not the god of creation mentioned in the other story. He may have been as resplendent, confident, and wise as a heavenly spirit, but he was a flesh-and-blood human being. It was said he came from a small inland village a few miles from present day Capistrano and that his parents had come to this part of California from another land.

In this account, Chinigchinich was a teacher who schooled his people in the right way to live and taught them rituals to help them remember their traditions. He also taught them how to heal the sick and care for the injured, how to deal with drought and famine, and how to treat the bodies of the dead. When he himself grew old, and death was approaching, he told his followers not to bury him in a cemetery among other people. Instead, they were to take his body to a private place from which he could continue to watch over his people.

"When I die," said Chinigchinich, "I shall ascend above, to the stars, and from thence, I shall always see you. To those who have kept my commandments, I shall give all they ask of me, but those who obey not my teachings, nor believe them, I shall punish severely. I will send bears to bite, and serpents to sting, and they shall be without food, and have diseases that they may die."

Having uttered these words, the mortal Chinigchinich became immortal. He was now a god or, at least began to be worshipped as one. And, as Father Boscana noted, he was a jealous god who constantly handed out punishments to a people who could never quite meet his high expectations. As a god, it seems, Chinigchinich was very unlike the concerned and caring teacher he had been as a man. As a man he had tended to the sick, but as a god he could get very angry when provoked, angry enough to bring the world to the brink of utter destruction.

On one such occasion Chinigchinich unleashed the rainmaker spirit who caused the skies to open and heavy rains to pour down for days on end. It rained so much that the ocean overflowed and spread out across the land drowning everything and nearly everyone. No one was saved except for a few faithful people who took refuge on top of a mountain. The floodwaters eventually receded, and afterward, Chinigchinich promised to never again bring such a calamity upon the earth.

Father Boscana could not fail to notice the similarity between this flood story and the one told in the Old Testament of the Christian Bible. There were other similarities as well. The god of Christianity was, after all, a very jealous and occasionally vengeful one.

Over the years, Boscana no doubt asked himself repeatedly whether Chinigchinich had only been an imaginary spirit, a means of explaining the unexplainable such as droughts, floods, lightning, and the deadliness of venom. Or had he been a real, though quite extraordinary man, who like himself, had devoted his life to a spiritual quest? As likely as not, Boscana never answered the question, at least not to his own satisfaction. When he died in 1831 at Mission San Gabriel north of Los Angeles, Boscana was interred among the more than two thousand Indians, settlers, and monks buried in the cemetery there and not in a secret place.

CHAPTER 12

Ghost Lights over the Pacific

Many believe the coasts of California are haunted and that the ghosts of dead sailors walk the rugged shores near the very rocks that long ago claimed their ships and their lives. Ghost sightings have been reported on the beaches near Crescent City and Point Reyes in the north, below the cliffs of the Golden Gate near San Francisco, at Point Arguello to the west of Santa Barbara, at Point Fermin and Point Ventura near Los Angeles, beside the bay in San Diego, and in many other coastal locations. Seeing a ghost takes an active imagination, and Californians are often very imaginative. The fog also helps, and of course, there is plenty of that here, so an impressionable observer might expect to spot a spook or two now and then.

Ghost sightings are especially common near active lighthouses. This may be because, at night, the light from the beacons bounces off the fog or haze creating a spectral image. Or it may be because lighthouses are naturally mysterious places of the sort likely to attract ghosts. Sometimes the lighthouses themselves are ghost-like, and they go on shining and doing the good work of saving ships and lives even long after they have been torn down and their beacons snuffed out. There are several of these phantom lights along the California coast.

When boaters, fishermen, and sailors get lost in the often foggy channel off Santa Barbara, they are sometimes guided to safety by a light emanating from the cliffs above the city. Some of them say the light they followed came from a small house on the cliff with a tower sticking up through its roof. The captains of freighters and oil tankers passing Santa Barbara on their way to the wharves at San Pedro Harbor or San Diego swear that during the day they can sometimes see the building quite clearly and they have even noted these sightings in their logbooks. That is odd, because the government has not maintained an active lighthouse at Santa Barbara since way back during the era of ragtime and flappers when Calvin Coolidge was president of the United States. The descriptions they give fit those of a structure that was utterly destroyed in 1925 by one of the most powerful earthquakes ever to strike California—which, of course, is saying a lot.

The lighthouse in question was once one of the most beautiful and historic buildings in the entire state. Before the earthquake, there were many fine old buildings in Santa Barbara, some of them dating all the way back to the time of Spanish rule. Alas, more than a few of these were shaken down to their very foundations by the mighty temblor. Even so, Santa Barbara remains a glorious place to live and a highly attractive destination for travelers.

Located on the east side of a high thumb of rock extending southward into the sea, this graceful city is nearly unique among California coastal communities. It is one of the few places in the West where you can see the sun rise over the ocean. Anyone who takes an evening stroll on a western beach should expect to see the sun set over the Pacific, but that is not what happens here. In Santa Barbara the sun sets over the mountains—and rises over the ocean. This geographic oddity tends to confuse early rising tourists who may have to be reminded that they are not in Atlantic City.

The unusual characteristics of this stretch of California coast are all too familiar to the masters of freighters and passenger liners plying the waters of the Santa Barbara Channel, which trends mostly toward the east. It is easy to get lost in the waters, to mistake the north for the east, the south for the west, and any such confusion can quickly lead to disaster. Mariners navigating near shore must know their precise positions at all times, for sharp, hull-crushing rocks lurk just beneath the surface all along the coast.

Countless ships have been ruined here and their passengers, crews, and cargoes consumed by the waves. During the Gold Rush, these losses were especially horrific. In 1854, on the rocks not far to the west of Santa Barbara, the *Yankee Blade* was lost along with more than four hundred passengers and crew. Along the rugged shores to the south and beneath the cliffs of the Santa Barbara Channel Islands, dozens of other Gold Rush–era steamers and windjammers came to grief. No one knows precisely how many passengers and how much cargo and treasure went down with them.

The Santa Barbara Lighthouse was intended to make navigating these deadly waters at least a little safer. Built in 1856, it was one of a string of sixteen lighthouses established along the nation's 2,500-mile western seaboard during and just after the Gold Rush. Most were built using the same set of plans. A small, two-story stone house with a thirty-foot tower sticking straight up through the middle of its roof, it was nearly identical to the lighthouses at Point Loma, near San Diego, Point Pinos, near Monterey, Alcatraz Island in San Francisco, and several other navigational vital locations along the California coast.

Built at a cost of only $8,000—including its expensive imported prismatic glass lens—the little Santa Barbara Lighthouse was nonetheless a remarkably sturdy structure. It weathered nearly seventy years of rain, wind, and gale. However, California has violent weather, not just above the ground, but also below it, and the lighthouse was destined to fall victim to a subterranean storm.

Shortly before dawn on the morning of June 29, 1925, people all over Santa Barbara were thrown out of bed by a powerful shock. One of them was Albert Weeks, keeper of the Santa Barbara Lighthouse. He had difficulty getting to his feet, for the floor under him was in motion. The very ground beneath the building was moving, first this way and then that. Weeks forced himself up. He knew he had to act quickly to save his family.

As a lighthouse keeper, Weeks was used to dealing with emergencies of various sorts, although never one quite like this. He was used to getting up at all hours to tend the light, something he had done ever since he was a small boy. He had been born into a lighthouse family. His father kept the Point Conception Lighthouse to the west of Santa Barbara and members of his family still worked there and at other California lighthouses.

As it happened, several members of Weeks's family were staying at the lighthouse when the earthquake struck. They had all gathered in Santa Barbara the previous evening for a sort of reunion and afterward had taken up every available bed and bit of floor space. The place got so crowded with Weeks's relatives that the keeper had been kicked out of his own house. He had spent the night in a nearby storage shed, and that is where he was when the earth began to move.

Weeks rushed outside and ran to the swaying lighthouse. The walls of both the tower and the dwelling were already beginning to crumble, and he could see that the building had only a few seconds left. Acting on instinct and driven forward by adrenaline, he dashed into the house and herded his family out through the door and into the yard. No sooner had he rescued the last occupant than the structure began to groan and sag.

Moments later the heavy tower crashed down through the roof, and the walls of the building tilted forward and collapsed.

The lighthouse was too badly damaged to be repaired and was never rebuilt. Weeks was later assigned to duty at another California lighthouse, but he always regretted the loss of his job and home in Santa Barbara. Although he and his family had left the cliffs above the city behind, Weeks was convinced that a beneficent presence remained there. From time to time during his years in Santa Barbara, he had caught a brief glimpse of an old woman walking the grounds of the lighthouse. When he attempted to approach her or speak to her, however, she would vanish. Over the years, Weeks began to suspect that he had seen Julia Williams, the famous "Lighthouse Lady of Santa Barbara," who had served as keeper of the city's lighthouse for half a century. Williams had died in 1911.

Julia Williams came to Santa Barbara during the 1850s. Born in eastern Canada, she made the trip to California by sailing ship and by mule across the Isthmus of Panama. Once in Santa Barbara, she married Albert Williams, who had just been made keeper of the recently built Santa Barbara Lighthouse. When Williams was killed in an accident a few years later, she took over his duties. Julia Williams served as keeper of the Santa Barbara Lighthouse from about 1861, the year the Civil War began, until she passed away shortly before World War I, a stretch of fifty years. There are those who say she keeps the light to this day even though both she and the lighthouse she served

for so long are supposedly gone. Mariners passing by Santa Barbara or entering the city's harbor sometimes say they've seen an
old woman waving to them from the cliffs.

Another California ghost light is sometimes seen far to the
north of Santa Barbara off the coast of the Golden State's famed
redwood country. About six miles out in the Pacific off Crescent
City, not far from the border between California and Oregon,
a long, blade-like volcanic outcropping rises from the waves. In
1792, English explorer George Vancouver first noted this dangerous obstacle, which he named Dragon Rock. The name was
well chosen since, over the years, it has gutted the hulls of more
than a few vessels and claimed many mariners. Barely visible
in clear weather and not at all in stormy conditions or fog, the
Dragon destroys its victims without taking flight or breathing
fire. All it needs to do is lie there waiting for some hapless captain
to steer his ship too near its unyielding shores. The rock's name
was eventually changed to St. George Reef, no doubt a reference
to the mythical medieval knight said to have slain a dragon. In
this case, however, St. George kills ships and people, not drag-
ons, and most sailors regard it as a sea monster. Those aboard the
steamer *Brother Jonathan,* on July 31, 1865, certainly considered
this reef a monster—a merciless one.

Built in 1851, the *Brother Jonathan* was 220 feet long, 36
feet abeam, and more than 1,500 tons in displacement. A side-
wheeler, she was fast for vessels of that day and could make the
trip from her homeport of San Francisco to Vancouver in British

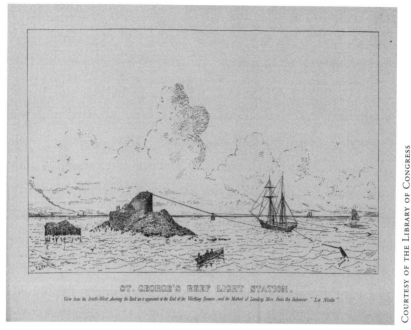

ST. GEORGE'S REEF LIGHT STATION.

View from the South-West, showing the Rock as it appeared at the End of the Working Season, and the Method of Landing Men from the Schooner. "La. Ninfa."

Built at great expense and cost of life during the late 1890s, the St. George Reef Lighthouse was intended to prevent deadly wrecks like the one that claimed the *Brother Jonathan* and hundreds of lives during an 1865 storm. The government shut down the lighthouse years ago, but passing mariners sometimes say they can still see its light.

Columbia in just three days. In late July of 1865, the *Brother Jonathan* was headed for Vancouver when she slammed head-on into a relentless gale. Only a few weeks earlier Confederate General Robert E. Lee had surrendered at Appomattox Court House, and President Abraham Lincoln had been assassinated. Given the slow pace of communication in those days, those onboard the *Brother Jonathan* may have only recently heard the news. As their vessel steamed steadily northward, they likely pondered these momentous events. Late on the afternoon of Monday,

July 31, however, their thoughts surely turned to more urgent matters. Lost in the storm, their captain had steered the vessel directly onto St. George Reef.

The impact tore a large hole in the steamer's hull, and within minutes the captain and his crew realized she was doomed. A valiant attempt was made to get the passengers safely off the ship, but though plenty of lifeboats were available, only three could be launched in the heavy seas. Two of these boats overturned and never made it to shore. Only one reached land in one piece, carrying eleven crewmen, five women, and three children to safety. Everyone else on the ship perished, including dozens of prospectors headed for Canada's Salmon River goldfields and a well-known San Francisco madam traveling to that same promising destination with seven of her young ladies. Also lost with the ship was Union General George Wright, and perhaps most ironic of all, Dr. Anson G. Henry, said to have been President Lincoln's closest friend.

The loss of the *Brother Jonathan* along with so many lives and notables generated a furor, and the government soon resolved that St. George Reef must be marked with a lighthouse. Ships approaching the rock were too far offshore to be warned by a lighthouse on land, so officials decided to build one directly over the rock. With the rather limited construction technology available at the time, this proved a daunting undertaking. It would take decades and more than $700,000 to complete the structure, making this in relative terms the most expensive lighthouse in history. Even so, mariners believed the big stone tower was well worth its hefty price. No one can say how many ships and lives it saved after its light first shone in 1892.

The St. George Reef Light served until 1972, when it was abandoned and replaced by a simple buoy. However, some lighthouses don't quit shining even after their keepers turn out the light. Occasionally, seamen report seeing the light, and record this in their logs, even though the beacon is no longer in operation. Some say this is because the glass at the top of the St. George Reef tower catches the last rays of the setting sun, while others insist that it is because the dragon's fires still burn.

BIBLIOGRAPHY

CHAPTER 1: WILL CALIFORNIA FALL INTO THE PACIFIC?

Kuzman, Dan. *Disaster! The Great San Francisco Earthquake and Fire of 1906.* New York: William Morrow, 2001.

Morris, Charles, ed. *The San Francisco Calamity by Earthquake and Fire.* Urbana: University of Illinois Press, 2002.

Turner, Patricia, ed. *1906 Remembered: Firsthand Accounts of the San Francisco Disaster.* San Francisco: Friends of the San Francisco Public Library, 1981.

CHAPTER 2: IS CALIFORNIA AN ISLAND?

McLaughlin, Glen, with Nancy H. Mayo. *The Mapping of California as an Island: An Illustrated Checklist.* Saratoga, Calif.: California Map Society, 1995.

Polk, Dora Beale. *The Island of California: A History of the Myth.* Spokane: Arthur H. Clark, 1991.

Virga, Vincent, and Ray Jones. *California: Mapping the Golden State through History.* Guilford, Conn.: Globe Pequot Press, 2010.

Chapter 3: House of Mystery

Anderson, Cynthia. *The Winchester Mystery House: The Mansion Designed by Spirits.* San Jose: The Winchester Mystery House, 1997.

Blanchard, Matt. "Build or Die: The Story of Sarah Winchester." Winchester Mystery House Press Release, 04/30/2009.

Madis, George, *The Winchester Book.* Houston: Art and Reference House, 1971.

Chapter 4: Did William Randolph Hearst Get Away with Murder?

Davies, Marion. *The Times We Had: Life with William Randolph Hearst.* Indianapolis: Bobbs-Merrill, 1975.

Granlund, Miles. *Blondes, Brunettes and Bullets.* New York: Van Rees Press, 1957.

Lynn, Kenneth. *Charlie Chaplin and His Times.* New York: Simon and Schuster, 1997.

Nasaw, David. *The Chief: The Life of William Randolph Hearst.* Boston: Houghton Mifflin, 2000.

Wilkerson, Marcus M. *Public Opinion and the Spanish-American War: A Study in War Propaganda.* Baton Rouge: Louisiana State University Press, 1932.

CHAPTER 5: WHERE IS THE HEAD OF ZORRO?

Curtis, Sandra. *Zorro Unmasked: The Official History.* Los Angeles: Hyperion Books, 1998.

Dooley, Garry. *The Zorro Television Companion.* North Carolina: McFarland, 2005.

Starr, Kevin. *California: a History.* New York: Modern Library, 2007.

Thorton, Bruce. *Searching for Joaquin, Myth Murrieta, and the History of California.* New York: Encounter Books, 2003.

CHAPTER 6: SHIPS AFLOAT ON SAND AND FOG

Belden, Burr, and Mary DeDecker. *Death Valley to Yosemite: Frontier Mining Camps & Ghost Towns.* California: Spotted Dog Press, 2005.

Chandler, Robert. *California: an Illustrated History.* New York: Hippocrene Books, 2004.

DeBuys, William. *Salt Dreams: Land and Water in Low-Down California.* Albuquerque: University of New Mexico Press, 1999.

CHAPTER 7: PEOPLE WHO EAT PEOPLE

Johnson, Kristin, ed. *Unfortunate Emigrants: Narratives of the Donner Party.* Logan: Utah State University Press, 1996.

Jones, Ray, and Joe Lubow. *Disasters and Heroic Rescues of California*. Guilford, Conn.: Globe Pequot Press, 2006.

McGlashan, C. F. *History of the Donner Party: A Tragedy of the Sierra*. Palo Alto, Calif.: Stanford University Press, 1940.

Unruh, John. *The Plains Across: The Overland Emigrants and the Trans-Mississippi West, 1840–60*. Urbana: University of Illinois Press, 1993.

CHAPTER 8: THE RAINMAN WHO FLOODED SAN DIEGO

Jenkins, Garry. *The Wizard of Sun City: the strange true story of Charles Hatfield, the rainmaker who drowned a city's dreams*. New York: Thunder's Mouth Press, 2005.

Patterson, Thomas W. "Hatfield the Rainmaker." *Journal of San Diego History, San Diego Historical Society Quarterly*. 16(4): Winter 1970.

Quinn, Heather. "Lake Morena County Park." *The San Diego Union-Tribune*, EZ.1., June 21, 2008.

Rasmussen, Cecilia. "'Cloud Coaxer' had a stormy career in parched deserts," *Los Angeles Times*, May 6, 2001.

Spence, Clark C. *The Rainmakers: American "Pluviculture" to World War II*. Lincoln, Neb.: University of Nebraska Press, 1980.

Van Deerlin, Lionel. "City's Water Woes Have a History." *The San Diego Union-Tribune*, p. B9, October 18, 2007.

Yellis, William. "Meet Charles Hatfield, the rainmaker of San Diego." San Diego News Network, June 10, 2009.

CHAPTER 9: GUNFIGHT AT MUSSEL SLOUGH

Beers, T. *Gunfight at Mussel Slough: Evolution of a western myth.* Santa Clara, Calif.: Santa Clara University, in conjunction with Heyday Books, Berkeley, Calif., 2004.

Brown, Richard Maxwell. *No Duty to Retreat: Violence and Values in American History and Society.* New York: Oxford University Press, 1991.

Chambers, Mary E. "Pioneers in Mussel Slough: A Lady's Experience," *Visalia Weekly Delta,* June 4, 1880. Reprinted in Beers, pp. 69-74.

Krieger, D. "Mussel Slough Was A Great Tragedy In History." *San Luis Obispo Tribune,* p. B4, April 8, 2001.

"Mussel Slough Tragedy." California Landmark 245, California Historical Landmarks in Kings County. Noe Hills Travel in California, a website: www.noehill.com/kings/cal0245.asp.

One of the Nineteen. "The Mussel Slough Difficulty." *San Francisco Argonaut,* 1881.

"The Railroad—Corruption, Deception, Violence All Part Of The Tale Of The Tracks." *Modesto Bee,* October 28, 2004.

"Railroad Robbers." *San Francisco Chronicle,* August 24, 1879.

Settlers' Committee. "An Appeal to the People." Pamphlet. Visalia, Calif: Delta Printing Establishment, 1880.

CHAPTER 10: CALIFORNIA'S VERY OWN PEARL HARBOR

"Battle of Los Angeles." California State Military Museum, A United States Army Museum Activity. www.militarymuseum .org/BattleofLA.html.

Bishop, Greg, Joe Oesterle, and Mike Marinacci. *Weird California.* New York: Sterling Publishing, 2006.

Craven, Wesley Frank, and James Lea Cate (eds.) "The Battle of Los Angeles" From *The Army Air Forces in World War II,* v.1. Washington, D.C.: Office of Air Force, 1983.

Hall, John. "The 'Great L.A. Air Raid' Actually Wasn't." *Orange County Register,* January 21, 2010.

Kurtus, Ron. "When the Japanese Bombed Santa Barbara." School for Champions website: www.school-for-champions .com/history/sbattack.htm.

"The Shelling of Ellwood." (n.d.) California State Military Museum, A United States Army Museum Activity. www .militarymuseum.org/Ellwood.html.

Young, Paul. *L.A. Exposed, Strange Myths and Curious Legends in the City of Angels.* New York: St. Martin's Griffin/Thomas Dunne Books, 2002.

CHAPTER 11: THE SHADOW GOD OF CALIFORNIA

Friar Geronimo Boscana. "Chinigchinich, a Historical Account of the Origin, Customs, and Traditions of the Indians at the Missionary Establishment of St. Juan Capistrano, Alta-California Called the Acagchemem Nation." Translated from the original Spanish manuscript by Alfred Robinson. From *Life in California* by Alfred Robinson. New York: Wiley and Putnam, 2010.

Kroeber, A. L. *Handbook of the Indians of California.* Bulletin 78, Smithsonian Institution Bureau of American Ethnology, 1925.

CHAPTER 12: GHOST LIGHTS OVER THE PACIFIC

Grant, John, and Ray Jones. *Legendary Lighthouses.* Guilford, Conn.: Globe Pequot Press, 2000.

Harrison, Tim and Ray Jones. *Lost Lighthouses: Stories and Images of America's Vanished Lighthouses.* Guilford, Conn.: Globe Pequot Press, 1998.

Jones, Ray. *The Lighthouse Encyclopedia.* Guilford, Conn.: Globe Pequot Press, 2004.

INDEX

ABOUT THE AUTHORS

RAY JONES

Ray Jones is a historian, author, and publishing consultant living in Pebble Beach California. He has written more than thirty books on topics ranging from dinosaurs to country stores, but is probably best known for his lighthouse travel guides and histories. Published by Globe Pequot Press in 2004, his award winning *Lighthouse Encyclopedia* is widely regarded to be the best and most informative volume on the subject. He has also written a number of PBS companion books including *Niagara Falls: An Intimate Portrait,* published in 2006 also by Globe Pequot Press.

JOE LUBOW

Joe Lubow, formerly Merrill College Librarian and Fellow at the University of California at Santa Cruz, has been an editor and author for more than twenty-five years. His writing has focused mainly on California history, living, and travel. His books with Globe Pequot Press include *Choose a College Town for Retirement* and, more recently, *Disasters and Heroic Rescues of California,* which he cowrote with Ray Jones. Along with writing and editing, Joe spends most of his nights surrounded by books and periodicals as the evening supervisor of the Library at California State University Monterey Bay.